Turning Points in Middle Schools

With love and respect, we dedicate this book to the thousands of young adolescents and their teachers who have impacted our professional careers and touched our lives, thereby contributing to the development of this book.

Turning Points in Middle Schools

Strategic Transitions for Educators

Mary M. Gallagher-Polite
Lela DeToye
John Fritsche
Nanci Grandone
Charlotte Keefe
Jacqueline Kuffel
Jodie Parker-Hughey

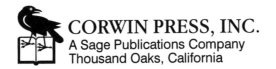
CORWIN PRESS, INC.
A Sage Publications Company
Thousand Oaks, California

For information address:

Corwin Press, Inc.
A Sage Publications Company
2455 Teller Road
Thousand Oaks, California 91320
E-mail: order@corwin.sagepub.com

SAGE Publications Ltd.
6 Bonhill Street
London EC2A 4PU
United Kingdom

SAGE Publications India Pvt. Ltd.
M-32 Market
Greater Kailash I
New Delhi 110 048 India

Printed in the United States of America

Library of Congress Cataloging-in-Publication Data

Main entry under title:

Turning points in middle schools: Strategic transitions for educators
   / Mary Gallagher-Polite . . . [et al.].
      p.   cm.
   Includes bibliographical references.
   ISBN 0-8039-6295-9 (acid-free paper).   —   ISBN 0-8039-6296-7
(pbk.: acid-free paper).
      1. Middle schools—United States.   2. Middle school teachers—
United States.   3. Middle school students—United States.
I. Gallagher-Polite, Mary.
LB1623.5.T87   1996
373.2'36—dc20   95-50169

This book is printed on acid-free paper.

96 97 98 99   10 9 8 7 6 5 4 3 2 1

Corwin Press Production Editor: Tricia K. Bennett

Contents

Preface

Hello, readers. You are about to take a 9-month journey and become actively engaged in the fictitious school community that we call Dewey Middle School. During the journey, key issues in middle grades education will be identified, explored, and even debated. First, readers will meet students who are in early adolescence (10-14 years old). This will provide an opportunity for readers to reflect about the unique characteristics of this age group. In Chapter 2, we focus on key elements of middle school, such as flexible scheduling, interdisciplinary learning, teacher-based guidance, and parent-community relations. From middle school philosophy, we move to program issues in Chapter 3 and instructional issues in Chapter 4. In Chapter 5, we present challenges outside the classroom, and Chapter 6 brings the school year to an end.

As you progress along your journey as readers, you will meet and hear the voices of the students, teachers, administrators, and parents that collectively make up the school community. Dewey is located in a city that is in transition, struggling to keep its traditions while keeping up with our fast-changing society. As in most cities and towns in the United States, the community wants its schools to be above average and progressive, but not *too* progressive.

The purpose of focusing on one fictitious school is twofold: to give readers a sense of cohesiveness and to present the application of middle school philosophy in a realistic manner. As readers will discover, Dewey has its successes and its disappointments. It is not a perfect school but one that is ever changing. Although Dewey is a fictitious school, it is, we believe, representative of the many schools across the nation on a journey to develop needs-responsive programs for young adolescents—a journey that has no final destination. Dewey is a collective vision of the schools in which we have taught, consulted, and completed research. This school is made up, but it is real.

The stories we tell about Dewey Middle School have been conceptualized around recommendations from the 1989 report *Turning Points: Preparing American Youth for the 21st Century.* In this landmark work, the Carnegie Council on Adolescent Development developed the following recommendations to guide schools in their work of developing needs-responsive programs for young adolescents:

1. *Create small communities for learning* where stable, close, mutually respectful relationships with adults and peers are considered fundamental for intellectual development and personal growth. The key elements of these communities are schools-within-schools, or houses; students and teachers grouped together as teams; and teacher-based guidance through small group advisories that ensure that every student is known well by at least one adult.

2. *Teach a core academic program* that results in students who are literate, including in the sciences, and who know how to think critically, lead a healthy life, behave ethically, and assume the responsibilities of citizenship in a pluralistic society. Youth service to promote values for citizenship is an essential part of the core academic program.

3. *Ensure success for all students* through elimination of tracking by achievement level, promotion of cooperative learning, flexibility in arranging instructional time, and adequate resources (time, space, equipment, and materials) for teachers.

4. *Empower teachers and administrators* to make decisions about the experiences of middle grade students through creative control by teachers over the instructional program linked to greater responsibilities for students' performance; governance committees that

assist the principal in designing and coordinating schoolwide programs; and autonomy and leadership within subschools, or houses, to create environments tailored to enhance the intellectual and emotional development of all students.

5. *Staff middle grade schools with teachers who are expert at teaching young adolescents* and who have been specially prepared for assignment to the middle grades.

6. *Improve academic performance through fostering the health and fitness* of young adolescents, by providing a health coordinator in every middle grade school and ensuring access to health care, counseling services, and a health-promoting school environment.

7. *Reengage families in the education of young adolescents* by giving families meaningful roles in school governance, communicating with families about the school program and students' progress, and offering families opportunities to support the learning process at home and at the school.

8. *Connect schools with communities* to share responsibility for each middle grade student's success through identifying service opportunities in the community, establishing partnerships and collaborations to ensure students' access to health and social services, and using community resources to enrich the instructional program and opportunities for constructive after-school activities. (pp. 9-10)

Most of the stories you will read on your journey do not include solutions to the problems encountered. Where solutions are presented, they may not be acceptable to individual readers. This strategy is intended to stimulate discussion and debate. At the end of each story, we list open-ended questions and activities, recommended readings, and a chart depicting the *Turning Points* (Carnegie Council on Adolescent Development, 1989) recommendations addressed in the story. We suggest that you keep a journal to note your ideas and thoughts along the way.

As you take your journey with the Dewey community, you will encounter forks in the road, places that may become turning points for you. Each fork will provide an opportunity for you to reflect and, hopefully, to grow. As you travel with Dewey through the turning points they encounter as they build a needs-responsive school, we hope that you too will learn more about what to change, how to change, and when to change, so that you can help orchestrate strategic transitions in schools for young adolescents.

Enjoy your trip.

Reference

Carnegie Council on Adolescent Development. (1989). *Turning points: Preparing American youth for the 21st century.* New York: Carnegie Corporation.

Introduction

The Community

Dewey Middle School is located on the west side of Oakdale, a community of 105,000, which has a proud history that dates back to the early 1800s. The central city has retained much of its original architecture and character due to new residents buying downtown property for historical renovations. Combined with the more modern, recent additions, the landscape of the community combines the best of the old and the new. People are proud to live and work in Oakdale and often live out their lives in the neighborhood where they grew up.

Oakdale College and the city's active arts council provide residents with a variety of cultural and educational opportunities. The city's extensive park system includes over 1,000 acres of recreational space for swimming, boating, and fishing. The recently completed science center, which boasts an Omnimax theater, consistently draws large crowds, as does the city's zoo, botanical garden, and antique center in the historic downtown section. Both blue-collar and white-collar employment are available in Oakdale's

light industries, various small and large businesses, and professional services. Agriculture continues to be a major occupation on surrounding
family farms, which produce corn, wheat, and soybeans. The relocation of
the headquarters of a major agricultural processing firm has brought many
new residents to Oakdale, and more are anticipated in the coming years. New
housing developments have sprung up across the community, with large
growth expected to continue on the west side.

The School District

The Oakdale Community Unit School District No. 14 serves approximately
12,500 students in prekindergarten through Grade 12 in the district's 3
comprehensive high schools, 3 middle schools, and 15 elementary schools.
Private and parochial schools in the community add to the options available
for children in Oakdale. Relationships between schools is friendly but
competitive.

Dr. Charles D. Bassert was hired as the Oakdale superintendent 5 years
ago when population increases meant more facilities were needed. Although this is his first superintendency, his prior experience in a neighbor-
ing district as an associate superintendent had earned him a reputation as
a visionary, collaborative leader. The community felt it was a real victory
when they stole him away, and although most of the residents in the community remain satisfied with his leadership, some are growing concerned
that his innovative philosophy is getting out of hand. The recent school
board election brought two new members to the board of education, Joseph
Kridle and Maude Mason, both with well-known agendas to oust Bassert
and hire a more conservative superintendent. They used the recent slight
decline in student test scores and graduation rates as the platform for their
position and won out over those who argued that scores were still above
the national average and there was no need for alarm.

Bassert believes in site-based management and therefore has a "lean
and mean" central office staff. Several administrative positions have been
eliminated in the past 3 years as he moved more and more decisions to the
building level. The remaining central office administrators act as a support
team for the district's building principals, who now have the lion's share
of work to do in all areas of school leadership and management. The recent
addition of a coordinating council at each building to oversee the functions
of the building and work with the building administrative staff to determine

budget and program, has created some anxiety in the district but the superintendent is determined to make a site-based system work in Oakdale.

The Building

One of three schools that serve students in Grades 6, 7, and 8, Dewey is the only middle school that has implemented more than the name. When sixth graders were moved to the junior high schools 4 years ago due to increasing enrollment across the district, only Dewey implemented middle school philosophy and practices. Although Bassert encouraged both Bloom Middle School and Tyler Middle School to embrace the middle school concept, the building administrators and coordinating councils supported the continuation of the traditional junior high programs that were well established at both sites. The Dewey staff initiated a transition plan, however, in part due to the appointment of Jane Byers as principal 4 years ago, and the school is well on its way to becoming a fully functioning middle school.

With an enrollment of 990 students in Grades 6 to 8, Dewey is the largest of the three district middle schools and is the one located in the section of town that continues to increase in population. The building is now at capacity and if the present growth trend continues something will need to be done to alleviate overcrowding. But for now, at least, that decision can wait.

Staff

Jane Byers, the principal at Dewey, is a child-centered, people-oriented leader. Her leadership style is generally described as collaborative, but she is quite willing to become autocratic if decisions are made that are not in the best interest of young adolescents. She was appointed principal at Dewey 4 years ago after 10 years as an elementary school principal in the district. Most people expected Richard Hoff, the assistant principal at Dewey, to get the appointment, but the staff is generally pleased with what the new principal has been able to accomplish in 4 short years—except, of course, for Richard Hoff.

Richard Hoff has been at Dewey for 20 years, 10 years as a teacher and 10 years as the assistant principal. Although he will be eligible for retirement in 5 years, he fought hard to win the Dewey principalship 4 years

Table I.1   Dewey Middle School Interdisciplinary Team Organization

Core Grade 6

Lean and Green	Harriet Plumber*	Math/Science
	John Graber	Social Studies/Language Arts
Pink Pistols	Shonte Myler*	Math/Science
	Colleen Hunt	Social Studies/Language Arts
Red Rascals	Mike Stiles*	Math/Social Studies
	Judy McKay	Science/Social Studies
	Kathleen Poppert	Language Arts/Social Studies
Gray Go-Getters	Wendell Jones*	Social Studies/Math
	Jill Wyers	Science/Math
	Jason McCowen	Language Arts/Math

Core Grade 7

Cranberries	Mac Delvanovich*	Science/Language Arts
	Hillary Weston	Math/Language Arts
	Bob Knoble	Social Studies/Language Arts
The Yellow Fellows	Ken Wilson*	Science
	Mary Allen	Language Arts
	Gayle Huin	Social Studies
	Bill Walker	Math
Golden Gators	Ray Brown*	Social Studies
	Nick Santino	Language Arts
	Nicole Chipperd	Math
	Connie Jackson	Science
	Priscilla Mac	Special Education Resource
Pink Pride	Sharon Becker*	Social Studies
	Martha Docweiler	Math
	Rita Restino	Science
	Paul Smith	Language Arts

Core Grade 8

Blue Angels	Jenny Mills*	Language Arts
	Tim Jones	Science
	Bill Morris	Social Studies
	Sue Walker	Math
Purple Paradise	Emily Pritchart*	Language Arts
	Kristen Baker	Language Arts, student teacher
	Jack Caulder	Science
	Barbara Peck	Math
	Lea Kowalski	Social Studies
	Lou Raningly	Special Education Resource
Hunters Green	Ed Matzler*	Social Studies
	Linda McCarthy	Language Arts

Table I.1   Continued

	Leslie Green	Math
	Chris Collier	Science
Lime Slime	Jennifer Nelson*	Math
	Suzanne Wacher	Social Studies
	Jeffrey Venner	Language Arts
	Norm Albert	Science
Encore Team		
Sparkling Specials	Jim Johnson*	Industrial Arts
	Gretchen Lipson	Art
	Carl Butler	Music
	Cindy Lopez	Instrumental Music
	Brenda Tiggs	Home Economics
	Melanie Michels	French
	Stanley Hadley	Spanish
	Nancy Evert	Physical Education
	Mark Lyden	Physical Education
	May Spencer	Media Director
Special Education		
Tangerines	Sandy Lasko*	Behavior Disorder
	Liz Rogers	Learning Disability Resource
	Margene Craft	Learning Disability Resource
	Tom Watson	Educable Mentally Handicapped

NOTE: * Denotes team leader.

ago. He believes that his disagreements with the superintendent were, at least in part, the reason he lost out to Jane Byers.

Ted Barrett, a 30-year-old in his second year as counselor, is loved by all in the school. Staff and students alike feel comfortable with him and the way he sees his role as a child and family advocate. He works tirelessly to link students and their families to Oakdale's social service agencies when help is needed and often has to use his people skills to bring harmony to the growing rift between Jane Byers and Richard Hoff.

Vickie Ardbright, a 20-year-veteran as counselor, sees her role at Dewey quite differently. She prefers paperwork and will go to great lengths to avoid one-on-one counseling with students. She takes pride in her reputation for quiet efficiency and is happy when she can stay in her office at her computer.

The teaching staff is listed above in Table I.1.

Questions for Discussion and Activities

1. What aspects of the community do you think are important to understand Dewey Middle School in context?
2. Given what you know about the Oakdale School District and superintendent, develop a 5-year district improvement plan. What issues are likely to surface in the district in the next 5 years?
3. Write a mission statement for Dewey Middle School. Develop goals and objectives for the school, along with a motto, logo, and school song that represent your current understanding of the school.
4. Analyze the interdisciplinary team organization at Dewey.
   a. Given a student population of 990, what would you estimate the average class size to be?
   b. Why have two-member, three-member, and four-member core teams?
   c. Review the disciplines taught by teachers in each team. Discuss the advantages and disadvantages of each team's organization.
   d. Discuss ways teachers can be placed on interdisciplinary teams in a school.
   e. How could the encore team be reconfigured? Is this organizational structure effective?
   f. Debate the pros and cons for a self-contained special education team.
5. What do you know about the academic program at Dewey from a review of the interdisciplinary team organization?
6. Take a learning style inventory (Kolb, 1976) or personality type inventory (Keirsey & Bates, 1984; Myers & Briggs, 1976). How could information from these types of instruments be used to place teachers on teams and for team development?
7. Develop a list of questions regarding the principal, the assistant principal, the counselors, and the teachers at Dewey presented in the school overview. What issues do you expect to emerge in the stories in the school? What interpersonal dynamics are likely to arise in relationships between the various individuals and groups in the school?

Relationship to Turning Points Recommendations

- Create small communities for learning
- Teach a core academic program

Recommended Reading

Clark, S., & Clark, D. (1987). *Restructuring the middle level school: Implications for school leaders.* New York: State University of New York Press.

George, P., & Alexander, W. (1993). *The exemplary middle school.* New York: Harcourt Brace Jovanovich.

Irvin, J. (Ed.). (1992). *Transforming middle level education: Perspectives and possibilities.* Boston: Allyn & Bacon.

Muth, K., & Alvermann, D. (1992). *Teaching and learning in the middle grades.* Boston: Allyn & Bacon.

Wiles, J., & Bondi, J. (1993). *The essential middle school.* New York: Macmillan.

References

Keirsey, D., & Bates, M. (1984). *Please understand me: Character and temperament types.* Del Mar, CA: Prometheus Nemesis.

Kolb, D. (1976). *Learning style inventory.* Boston: McBer.

Myers, I. B., & Briggs, K. C. (1976). *Myers-Briggs type indicator* (reprint). Palo Alto, CA: Consulting Psychologists Press.

About
the Authors

Lela DeToye, Ed.D., is an Associate Professor and Curriculum and Instruction Department Chair at Southern Illinois University at Edwardsville. She is project director for the Mississippi Valley Writing Summer Institute at SIUE and works with schools on language arts and integrated curriculum development.

John Fritsche, Ed.D., is an Associate Professor and Education Department Chair at Illinois College in Jacksonville, Illinois. In addition to supervising student teachers and teaching curriculum and middle school courses, he is active in developing school partnerships that enhance minority student achievement and cultural diversity.

Nanci Grandone, Ed.S., is a guidance counselor for the Alton Community Unit School District at North Middle School in Godfrey, Illinois. She has served as a supervisor for student teachers at Southern Illinois University at Edwardsville and has been a training specialist and coordinator for a number of public agencies.

Charlotte Keefe, Ed.D., is an Associate Professor of Special Education at Texas Women's University in Denton, Texas. She is an active author and researcher on topics related to special education, inclusion, assessment, and whole language instruction for special learners.

Jacqueline Kuffel, M.S., is a middle school teacher at Mascoutah Middle School in Mascoutah, Illinois. She was instrumental in the recent change process at her school and is active in developing interdisciplinary units as a member of a three-person core team.

Jodie Parker-Hughey, M.A., is a consultant with HRStrategies in St. Louis, Missouri. Her work in industrial and organizational psychology led to a graduate student award at Southern Illinois University at Edwardsville, where she completed her thesis on preservice teacher portfolio assessment.

Mary Gallagher-Polite, Ph.D., is an Associate Professor of Educational Administration at Southern Illinois University at Edwardsville. She is President of the Association of Illinois Middle-Level Schools and editor of the *AIMS Journal.* She works with teachers and administrators in several states on middle school reform.

Meeting the Dewey Community

1

Story 1:

A Hot August Afternoon

On August 25, it is hot in the Dewey Middle School teachers' lounge. The students have just left the building after their first half day of school, and teachers are gathering in the teachers' workroom before a faculty luncheon and opening day in-service session. Emily Pritchart, an eighth-grade language arts teacher and team leader, sits alone at a long table looking over her team roster when she notices Richard Hoff, the assistant principal, enter the room with the new school board member, Joseph Kridle.

Hoff: Good afternoon, Emily. Have you met Mr. Kridle from the board of education?

Pritchart: Mr. Kridle. [nods her head] Welcome to Dewey Middle School.

Kridle: Middle school—I just can't get used to calling Dewey a middle school. When I went here it was Dewey Junior High School. And we were proud of it. What subject do you teach, Ms. Pritchart?

Pritchart: I teach *students* language arts.

Kridle: Well, lord knows students need help in that area. Back to the basics, that's what I say. Heavy doses of grammar, usage, and spelling, that's what kids need.

Hoff: [with a smirk] Mr. Kridle, Emily here is experimenting with a mixed-ability group in her language arts classes. She feels that students shouldn't be grouped according to ability.

Kridle: What? Well, just see that you don't dummy down the curriculum. Dewey prides itself on high achievement scores.

Vickie Ardbright, a counselor at Dewey, enters the room on the end of Kridle's comment on test scores.

Ardbright: What's that about test scores? I've been preparing a database of student test scores to trace a student's scores since kindergarten. I'm wondering if each team should have this testing information on each student at the beginning of the year. That way they'll know what to expect from their students.

Hoff: Well, I'm more interested in looking at progress in students from year to year. We need to monitor whether this middle school experiment is really working for our students.

Pritchart: The middle school concept looks at the young adolescent with a broader lens than just their academic progress, Mr. Hoff.

Kridle: I'm sure we're all aware of that, Ms. Pritchart, but the bottom line is academics and preparing these kids for high school.

Ardbright: Speaking of getting kids ready for high school, I can't keep my walk-in advising schedule for several weeks, Mr. Hoff. I need that time to start registering the eighth graders for their freshman classes.

Mike Stiles, a sixth-grade team leader enters the room and the conversation.

Stiles: No walk-in advising? Gee, Vickie, you know how it is at the beginning of the year, some of our sixth graders are going to need some help in adjusting to middle school. They need someone other than their teachers to talk with about some of this stuff.

Ardbright: I thought that's what advisory is for. Besides, this stuff has to be done.

Kridle: Advisory? What's that?

Pritchart: All students at Dewey are placed in small groups of 12 to 15 for teacher-based guidance. These groups meet daily to help our students deal with the normal emotional and social turmoil of young adolescence. Teachers get to know their advisory students well and serve as an advocate for them in the school. Advisory is a key component of an effective middle school, Mr. Kridle. I invite you to come and visit our advisory classes anytime to learn more about them.

Kridle: Advisory? Adjusting to middle school? Whatever happened to hard work and tough love? Come on, Mr. Hoff, show me where I'll be speaking to the faculty this afternoon. I need a few minutes to work on my speech.

The teachers Martha Docweiler and Ed Matzler enter the room in time to overhear this conversation about advising.

Docweiler: [to Ed Matzler] Forget about the kids, I'm the one who needs counseling.

Matzler: What's wrong, Martha? The new year's just beginning; it's too early to be depressed.

Docweiler: I guess I should retire. I just can't keep up with all of the changes around here. Advisory, co-curricular activities, teaming, block schedules. I just want to teach. And the kids, they're just not like they used to be.

Matzler: Well, I'll agree about some of that. It's been hard for me to adjust to some of the changes middle school has brought to Dewey. But I can't complain about teaming. I'm retiring at the end of the year, but teaming has made me feel differently about leaving. Before, teaching was such a lonely act. It had become routine and boring. Now, my teammates and I are really working together, planning instruction and teaching kids instead of just content. Teaching, for me, has become a whole new thing and I'm grateful to be ending my career on a positive note.

Docweiler: I wish I could say the same things about my team. It seems all we do is complain about kids and plan ways to gang up on them.

Matzler: Who complains about kids?

Docweiler: Now, don't you turn on me—I know, I do my share of complaining, but I've been around here a long time. Older teachers used to be treated with respect but . . .

Their conversation is drowned out by the loud bell that normally signals the end of lunch hour. Today, it signals the beginning of opening day in-service activities. The teachers file out of the workroom in small groups. They hold the key to the success or failure of Dewey Middle School. Most teachers at Dewey are excited about the beginning of the new year. Most are dedicated to their students and their profession, but some yearn for the olden days of Dewey Junior High. Together they'll forge the future of Dewey Middle School.

Questions for Discussion and Activities

1. Read between the lines—make a list of the various attitudes you hear being expressed by Dewey teachers the first day of school.
2. Make some predictions about how these various attitudes will affect the progress of Dewey as it moves toward becoming a fully functioning middle school.
3. Spend some time in the teachers' lounge at various schools. What do you hear? What points of view and topics are discussed?
4. What do you think is included in the "broader lens" that Emily Pritchart spoke of? Are academics the "bottom line"? Why or why not?

Relationship to Turning Points Recommendations

- Create small communities for learning
- Ensure success for all students

Recommended Reading

Dorman, B., Lipsitz, J., & Verner, P. (1985). Improving schools for young adolescents. *Educational Leadership, 42*(6), 44-49.

Epstein, J. L., & MacIver, D. J. (1990). *Education in the middle grades: Overview of national practices and trends.* Columbus, OH: National Middle School Association.

Fenwick, J. J. (1986). *The middle school years.* San Diego, CA: Fenwick Associates.

Irvin, J. (Ed.). (1992). *Transforming middle level education: Perspectives and possibilities.* Boston: Allyn & Bacon.

Story 2:

All Aboard

"Can you believe that summer is over, and we have to go back to school again?" Jimmy asked his friend as they waited at the bus stop for a ride on the first day of a new school year at Dewey Middle School.

"Yeah, summer went way too fast, but at least this year we are in eighth grade. We'll rule over those puny sixth graders," Mark laughed.

"Speaking of sixth graders, here comes a couple of them. It seems that they keep getting smaller and skinnier each year. We weren't that skinny when we were in sixth grade," Jimmy exclaimed.

"You're right. We were much bigger and of course cooler," Mark boasted.

Meanwhile, across the street, Sarah and Christy didn't feel so confident.

"Does my hair look okay? How do I look?" Sarah was nervous and wanted to make sure she made a good impression on her first day at Dewey.

"You look fine," Christy replied. "How do I look?" Christy too was concerned about being noticed and making a positive impression on her first day.

"You look great, too. It would be nice to have the eighth graders notice us, but I think it is gonna be tough," commented Sarah aloud. Both girls silently fought their anxiety while thinking that they surely didn't compare with the older girls who were more poised and more developed than they were.

"There is this cute seventh grader that lives down the block from me. His name is Matt, and, boy, is he cute! He looks so much older than those dumb sixth graders. I sure hope he talks to me this year, because he even knows my name. Oh my gosh, here he comes! Are you sure that I look okay?" Sarah anxiously asked.

"Yes, Sarah, you look great. Just stay there and smile and maybe he will come over and talk to you," Christy replied.

Matt and his buddy Steve walked up to the bus stop wearing their latest athletic finery. They stood next to the group of eighth graders who had gathered at the corner but didn't talk to them because they were known at school as a rough crowd. Everyone knew they spent their time smoking, drinking, and messing with drugs, and Matt and Steve were definitely not interested in that.

"Hey, Steve, did you catch the baseball game last night? It sure was incredible. It would be so great to be able to play ball like that," Matt exclaimed.

"Yeah, what a great game, but hey, have you gotten a look at those girls over there? They must be sixth graders because I have never seen them before. They are kinda cute, especially the redhead," Steve said.

"That's only Sarah, she lives right by me. I never thought she was cute, but her friend is not bad," Matt replied.

"You gotta be kidding me. She's great! She sure beats any of the girls in our class. We have some of the nerdiest girls—hey, speak of the devil, here comes the queen nerd and her best friend now."

"I am so excited about being in seventh grade. We get to study American history, algebra, and science and read all of those great books in language arts," Lisa exclaimed to her best friend Kathy.

"I know. I can't wait. We're so lucky to be on the same team, plus we get to be with Mr. Wilson, and he is a great teacher," Kathy replied.

"Everyone says how hard his science class is, but I bet he is not that hard. All it takes is some studying and we can still make straight As. I'm not going to ruin my perfect record of all As," Lisa boasted.

"Yeah, me too. I don't think we should have any problems, because we are the smartest kids in our class," Kathy exclaimed.

As the bus pulled to a stop, it was clear that being the last stop meant seats were at a premium. Jimmy and Mark walked on first and headed straight for the back of the bus. Lisa and Kathy walked on next, and a couple of their friends had saved them seats in the first row. Christy and Sarah nervously walked on next. They did not recognize anybody, and there were no empty seats left together. Matt and Steve walked on last. They found a couple of seats with their buddies and immediately started talking about the basketball game that they were planning for after school. At the back of the bus, Jimmy and Mark turned to make fun of the two newcomers.

"Hey, Mark, look at those two little girls. They must be lost. They have no idea where to sit. Hey, there's room back here for you two. Come on back here with us," Jimmy yelled.

And as the laughter on the bus grew, the driver's voice rose above it all with the command that everyone be seated so they could proceed on the way to school.

The first day of middle school had begun.

Questions for Discussion and Activities

1. What are the stereotypes of young adolescents that are brought out in this story? What other important characteristics of young adolescents are not discussed in this story?
2. What are your own personal biases about young adolescents?
3. How can these stereotypes and characteristics be addressed in the school setting?
4. Interview middle schoolers to get their thoughts and feelings about themselves and school.
5. Develop an annotated bibliography of adolescent literature related to characteristics of kids and issues for kids in schools.

Relationship to Turning Points Recommendations

- Ensure success for all students
- Prepare teachers for the middle level

Recommended Reading

Elkind, D. (1990). *The hurried child.* Boston: Addison-Wesley.

Kramer, L. (1992). Young adolescents' perceptions of school. In J. Irvin (Ed.), *Transforming middle level education: Perspectives and possibilities* (pp. 28-45). Boston: Allyn & Bacon.

Milgram, J. (1992). A portrait of diversity: The middle level student. In J. Irvin (Ed.), *Transforming middle level education: Perspectives and possibilities* (pp. 16-27). Boston: Allyn & Bacon.

Muth, K., & Alvermann, D. (1992). *Teaching and learning in the middle grades.* Boston: Allyn & Bacon.

Scales, P., & McEwin, K. (1994). *Growing pains: The making of America's middle school teachers.* Columbus, OH: National Middle School Association.

Stevenson, C. (1992). *Teaching ten- to fourteen-year-olds.* New York: Longman.

Story 3:

A Profile of a Seventh Grader

Jonathan never hesitated to inform anyone that the reason he thought the best time of the day was 3 o'clock in the afternoon was because school was over. Unless, of course, it was Saturday—the day he loved best. His performance in school gave no evidence of his feelings, however. Jonathan's first-quarter report card was as good as anyone at Dewey ever got—straight As with comments like "Good work habits," "Pleasure to have in class," "Displays good effort," "Actively participates in class," and "Good attitude!" from the teachers. Although Jonathan performed well, he generally thought he didn't learn much that was useful. He believed most of what was done in school could be accomplished in fewer days or, at least, in shorter days, which could begin around 10 in the morning as he liked to sleep in.

Jonathan's world revolved around sports. He looked forward each morning to sitting down with a bowl of his favorite cereal for that week and the sports section of the newspaper, which he studied for 20 minutes while eating. He examined the standings to see if there were changes. He knew the win-loss record of all the NBA teams and the average points per game of the star players from each team and was constantly projecting the outcomes of the next series of games. He had a subscription to *Sports Illustrated,* and he read the magazine each night before going to bed. Even though he would get one or two issues behind, he never read the latest issue until he had completed all the articles he had intended to read in all previous issues. He was careful to set aside time each evening to read from a magazine or book before going to sleep.

Jonathan loved basketball more than any other game. His began to play and develop an interest in the game when the Chicago Bulls won their first NBA championship. Successive championship seasons by this team earned his loyalty. He bought and read books about the players and fantasized about playing in the NBA some day. Jonathan spent hours alone shooting baskets and working on drills. He would rather play with someone else, but few of his friends shared his enthusiasm for the spirited competition that usually prevailed. Often, his invitations to friends were met with excuses, phone messages he left were never returned, and he ended up shooting baskets alone.

Jonathan worried about making Dewey's basketball team because he knew he was one of the shortest boys trying out. This bothered him a lot, especially when one boy who everyone knew would make the team coldly guaranteed that he would not make it. Jonathan doesn't think much about it now, but his father, who took him to the school on that Friday evening to check the list posted of boys who made the final cut, will always have the image burned in his mind of his 12-year-old son, handsome; self-assured; healthy; alive with enthusiasm, flexibility and a sense of humor, sitting next to him in the car crying in silent, choking, gasping sobs of disappointment after discovering he did not make the final cut for the basketball team.

It was difficult for Jonathan to cast off the disheartened and dejected feelings of not making the team, even though 45 other boys didn't make it either. The disappointment was very personal and he did not want to face anyone on the following Monday. To be a part of the team was important— even if he only sat on the bench.

Jonathan moved through the grieving process and slowly arrived at a new stage of optimism. He hadn't played basketball at home for a couple of weeks. He worked through his anger over attending all the tryout sessions and completing all the drills required although some who made the team didn't even show up for some of the tryout sessions. Assurance by the coach that grades would be looked at and teachers consulted before selecting the team had been the basis for his increased optimism and confidence and then a source of anger and grief. Jonathan knew the reports on his grades, attitudes, and conduct were good whereas one boy who made the team had been involved in fights in school this year and would probably be suspended. The coach selected two boys from Jonathan's academic team who were failing in some subjects and would be ineligible much of the season. It was hard to believe the coach didn't realize he had made a mistake in selecting these players, and because he was certain he just missed the cut, he remained hopeful that he would soon be summoned to join the team.

In the meantime, Dusty, a newly acquired friend, invited Jonathan to meet him at the YMCA to play basketball. A friendship was quickly established as the boys discovered common interests. Dusty was an only child who shared the same lunch period with Jonathan and hadn't made the team either. He told Jonathan that the coach said they should plan to go out for the eighth-grade team next year because they were among the next three boys to have made the team. They enjoyed getting together after school to trade NBA basketball cards or to play one-on-one or two-on-two if they could find two other boys available whose parents could drive them to someone's home.

Jonathan looked forward to weekends. He usually made arrangements to have someone overnight on Friday or Saturday, or he would stay overnight at another friend's home. The overnight routine almost always involved eating pizza, Nintendo game playing, listening to the latest popular CD, and watching a movie, intermixed with discussions on clothes, sports, movies, TV shows, and other kids. The movies the boys watched were usually R rated. Movies rated lower than PG-13 were not considered worth watching by anyone who considered himself mature.

Rarely is school a topic for discussion among Jonathan and his peers except in relation to what a teacher did that might be considered bizarre, odd, or peculiar. When the conversation was about other students, it centered on the "less upbeat" students, hostile students, the loners who serve as scapegoats in a group, or the teachers' pets.

Monday morning was Jonathan's least favorite day of the week. Although he rarely complained about school, he answered his parent's "How's school?" with "Fine" and hoped the conversation on school would end at that point. He disliked school and did complain on those days he had homework. Because he was taking a foreign language and a full complement of electives, he had no team study time. He always tried to get homework completed in school because he so hated bringing it home. When he does bring work home, he usually divides it into segments, doing a little immediately when he gets home while eating a snack, more after it gets too dark to play outside and before eating supper, and the rest after watching a couple of his favorite TV programs. He rarely needs help except to study for tests.

For Jonathan, the only rational part of school is the tests. A greater portion of his grade is based on tests than on any other kind of assignment. He has developed good skills for remembering the factual details teachers at Dewey like to test for. He likes the challenge and competition and thrives on getting good scores. The night before a test he always asks his mother or father to quiz him on the study sheets. Afterward, he rarely forgets to report to his parents the scores he received on the tests taken that week. He knows how much his parents like him to receive good grades and he has come to appreciate the reward they give him following a good report card. He is hoping this time they will be generous and get him one of the "starter" jackets worn by a lot of the kids at Dewey. He is worried he won't ever grow out of the "generic" jacket he has been wearing since fifth grade.

Clothes are important to Jonathan. This year he has paid more attention to what he wears and how frequently it is worn than ever before. If something was worn during one week, don't wear it the next week is the controlling norm among the preppy group at Dewey. Each morning, Jonathan places a pair of pants on the carpeted floor in his room and to explore possible combinations places different tops over the pants. If the selected combination seems questionable to him, he consults with his sister, a high school sophomore, who gives the final approval. Feeling positive his dress will draw no derisive remarks from a peer, he prepares for the challenge of another burdensome day at Dewey Middle School.

Questions for Discussion and Activities

1. Should extracurricular activities be used to motivate students to perform better academically?
2. Should extracurricular activities be used to motivate and build positive attitudes about school in disadvantaged or at-risk students?
3. Discuss the pros and cons of interscholastic sports versus intramural sports at the middle school level.
4. What makes a school a learner-centered school?
5. What is the role of friends for middle level learners?
6. Write a profile of yourself as a middle school student. Write a profile of a middle school student different from Jonathan. Share with members in your class.
7. Shadow a middle-level student and write a summary of your most interesting insights. Design and carry out an informal inquiry to learn about current middle-level student characteristics and attitudes.

Relationship to Turning Points Recommendations

- Ensure success for all students
- Prepare teachers for the middle level

Recommended Reading

Dorman, G., Lipsitz, J., & Verner, P. (1985). Improving schools for young adolescents. *Educational Leadership, 42*(6), 44-49.

Elkind, D. (1986). Stress and the middle grader. *School Counselor, 33*(3), 196-206.

Lipsitz, J. (1984). *Successful schools for young adolescents.* New Brunswick, NJ: Transaction Books.

Lounsbury, J. H., Marani, J. V., & Compton, M. F. (1980). *The middle school in profile: A day in the seventh grade.* Columbus, OH: National Middle School Association.

Stevenson, C. (1992). *Teaching ten- to fourteen-year-olds.* New York: Longman.

Embracing the
Middle School Way

2

Story 4:

What's So Great About Dewey?

As part of a research project underway at Oakdale College, George Davis, Professor of Educational Foundations, needed to interview good teachers in effective middle schools in the Oakdale region. One of the teachers on his list was Ed Matzler, a Dewey Middle School teacher who had the reputation of being one of the better teachers in the Oakdale School District.

Ed Matzler has spent his entire 30-year teaching career at Dewey. He is a social studies teacher and a strong advocate of the middle school movement. Because he believes so strongly that a faculty, administration, and parents should agree on a set of core beliefs to unite them in developing and carrying out the educational programs at Dewey, he was instrumental in the development of the following mission statement, which is displayed prominently in the entryway of the school.

Dewey Middle School is committed to providing its students, within an educationally positive atmosphere, a purposeful curriculum and activities that support the values of learning and democratic citizenship.

Thirty years ago, "teaching" at Dewey was quite different from today. In that time, Ed Matzler has experienced the introduction of the teaming concept, common planning times for teams of teachers, interdisciplinary teaching, cooperative learning strategies, and exploratory programs among numerous other innovations that have come and gone over the years. He is a walking advertisement for all these practices even though he admits how distressing it was at times for the faculty to make the transition from a junior high school to a middle school.

Ed Matzler is planning to retire after this school year. He is proud of his 30 years in the profession and looks back over his teaching career at Dewey with much contentment and satisfaction. He was thrilled to have the chance to discuss his career during an interview with George Davis.

Davis: What is so great about Dewey that caused you to remain for 30 years?

Matzler: You know, when I first started to teach I didn't even want to teach at Dewey. I wanted to teach at the high school. To tell the truth, I didn't even know there was such a thing as a junior high or a middle school, because there wasn't one where I grew up. It was a K through 8 school. They didn't have a position at the high school so they sent me to Dewey. I knew it was a school because I had been there to play basketball, but I had never paid much attention to it. I think that's where a lot of people are. They don't understand what the junior high or middle school "thing" is. I had no desire to teach sixth, seventh, or eighth grade, until I got into it. Then I found it was tremendous, especially the team concept.

Davis: Did you teach during the time seventh, eighth, and ninth grades were together?

Matzler: Yes, there were three junior highs throughout the city. Several teachers from Dewey were forced to go to a new junior high, which had been designed around the "open schools" concept. There was this huge open area, which drove teachers nuts, because you could be teaching here and 5 feet away was another teacher's class, and if he was a loud teacher, your students would be paying attention to him.

Davis: You mentioned "teaming." How was this notion introduced at Dewey?

Matzler: It was initiated by the teachers who came to Dewey from this open school. They had a beautiful setup. Each team had a room where the four teachers had their desks and a giant open space where they taught. The social studies, language arts, and math teachers were all in one area, and the science teachers were off in the science area. They could remove barriers and all 120 to 130 kids could meet in one large group. Or they could say, "I need language arts for two periods today." It was great because they had the physical setup to accommodate different needs. Of course, when they were moved to Dewey they were already tied into a system and wanted to do the same at Dewey. The more structured teachers like me fought it. The reason I fought teaming was because I thought it would take a lot of control away from me as a teacher, with my curriculum and my classroom. But it didn't. It was just the opposite, even though I was not with a real strong group the first year. No teacher in our group had ever team-taught before so we really didn't know what we were doing.

Gradually, as we worked our way through teaming we found out how good it could be. It was great for discipline. A teacher would say, "Well, he's doing the same thing in my room" or "Have you tried this?" or "Did you know that his mother has cancer?" It just made discipline so much easier, because if we had to talk to a kid, all four of us would talk to a kid. If parents were coming in they were facing four adults, not just one adult. So, right then, I saw that as a positive effect.

Then the language arts teacher and I began to coordinate our teaching. If we were in the Civil War she would have students do things like write diaries as if they had been in the war or as if they were parents writing to their son and all these different things while I was teaching about the Civil War. We had all this stuff we displayed everywhere. Field trips became far better because the four of us would talk about it. We had a science field trip that was outstanding. I had a social studies trip and we came up with a math trip where we took them to the shopping center. I thought I would hate it and it turned out to be super.

Soon after teaming began, however, we lost the teams because enrollment had gone down and we lost two teachers. I hated it that year. Later that year, the four chairmen of the departments were allowed to visit a middle school that had just gotten an award for team teaching. While there, we got our act together, came back and made a presentation, and the next year we got teaming back. It was at this same time that we began the transition into a middle school.

Davis: What did you not like about the year without teams?

Matzler: Discipline. Not that I particularly had discipline problems, but I had nobody to talk to. I did not know who had Johnny in science, language arts, or math. So I had to go and look up his record and go talk to them and ask, "How's he doing in your class? Field trips were almost nonexistent. You didn't take them because all the teachers had all these kids and there weren't any four teachers that had a certain group that could be selected for a trip. Either you took a trip by yourself or you didn't go. I took only one trip because it was too cumbersome. I had to get a bunch of parents to go along. The beautiful thing about taking students on a field trip as a team was that it was like a big family because we were doing things together. It was a bonding thing. We were trying to get the kids to pull together as a unit and field trips helped us to do that.

Davis: Was there any other way for your team to be distinct from other teams in the school?

Matzler: Well, the teams used to be called Team 1, Team 2, Team so on. The names of the teams were changed, however, because everyone thought that our team, Team 1, was better than Team 2 just because it was numbered Team 1. It was the teachers who thought this. So now the team names change each year based on a theme, such as "trees."

Davis: What are the advantages of having a theme?

Matzler: It gets the teams off to a good start at the beginning of the year by providing teams with a topic for planning an integrated interdisciplinary unit to begin the year with. Teams plan activities for the first weeks based on this theme and their name to help kids get to know all of their classmates and identify with the team. The activities are designed to provide an opportunity for all students to be successful and to receive some kind of recognition. It also demonstrates that the teachers on the team are working together toward the same common goals.

Last year our theme was trees. Our motto was "Like trees, Dewey students grow strong and tall." It was neat to see trees serve as a vehicle to study patterns in mathematics, or family trees in social studies, and poetry in language arts. Some pretty exciting learning took place those first several weeks.

Davis: How did Dewey go about establishing a total school identity?

Matzler: Through the mission statement we adopted as a middle school.

Davis: How was this developed?

Matzler: Each teacher submitted a mission statement without putting his or her name on it. Without discussing them, the faculty voted on them and narrowed them down to six or seven. Then we took those and discussed what each one meant and pulled the ideas together so the final mission statement pretty well says what we try to do.

Davis: With all the different personalities on Dewey's faculty, what causes the school to work so well?

Matzler: Not to make it too general, but every teacher's desire for the kids to get the very best education possible at Dewey is the main reason for the school functioning well. About 90% of the teachers have this philosophy. The teams do their best to translate that in their own way without getting involved in competing with other teams.

Davis: Did you ever find that there was competition between teams?

Matzler: Oh, yes. Competition among teachers was one thing in education that drove me nuts. When the issue of our being the best team because we were called Team 1 was being battled over, I said, "The only reason we are considered the best team is because we do things for kids." Somebody else said, "We do, too." I said, "No, you don't. You think you do, but you talk to the counselors. Every year we ask for some of the poorest kids and make them our projects to see if we can turn them around. How many of you ask for these kids just so you can work with them?"

We used to have this "spring fever" competition but had to do away with it because another team got too competitive when our team kept winning it. The only reason we kept winning it was because we let kids choose what they wanted to do and we encouraged them to participate because you got points for every kid that showed up. You also got points for every event you won. Every year all of our kids showed up.

We won the first 2 years because we would take our kids to the cafeteria and have them sign up on these big charts for the events they wanted to participate in and we guaranteed they would get to participate in at least one of their favorite events. Then we would take some of our rough kids—the tough, "wrong side of the track" kids—and made them team captains. I would talk to them and say, "This is your responsibility." Some of them were pretty good athletes. I think we won every year because we got every kid involved and made to feel valued.

The other teams never did real well because they weren't very organized. It became the thing with one team to beat us. My son was on that team, which is why I know this. But a lot of their kids got upset because the teachers wouldn't let them choose their own event. The teachers handpicked them for the events and put their best athletes in certain events to make sure they would win the event against us. When it was all over with, they thought they had beaten us. But there was a third team involved that had beaten them in certain places and when they added up the score all of a sudden it became apparent we had won again. Then, they went down and protested saying we had cheated. This brought an end to the spring fever competitions, because the faculty thought it had become too competitive among the teachers. But any time you are going to have teams you are going to have some competition.

Davis: Then would you consider this to be a negative aspect of teaming?

Matzler: No, I think it is part of our American culture to be competitive. Even some of the cooperative learning strategies we use at Dewey have a certain amount of competition incorporated into them.

Davis: What, then, do you see as some of the benefits of teaming?

Matzler: Teaming allows us to see other teachers' strengths and weaknesses. If you have a good team, you have a commitment to each other first and to your content second. I get a lot of my good ideas from the other teachers. In a team, you can say, "Try this with that kid." Because I taught social studies, I could take it and make it a social studies thing.

Teaming is good for kids because it was good for teachers. The most important thing in public schools are the kids, but right behind them are the teachers. Teachers have to be happy and administrators should do as much as they can to make the teachers' job easier. We know we aren't going to have a hundred thousand dollars in the bank or a new sports car to drive, but make sure we have good equipment to use and make sure we are supported when we do ask. For example, Dewey has good counselors. They would do anything for teachers and kids. That's important.

The parenting thing is another issue that makes teaming a positive factor for teachers. There is nothing scarier then to have mad parents come in and you are the only one there. We had one come in after Ms. McCarthy once, and the girl was wrong, and the parents came in all fit to kill, and they saw all four of us were there. They said, "We only want to talk to Ms. McCarthy." I was the team leader and responded, "No, you never talk to just Ms. McCarthy. We are a team and we all have your daughter and we all four have things to discuss with you about your daughter." She wasn't a bad girl, but she was sitting there quietly, and when it was over with, the mother was crying, and the daughter was crying, because the daughter had pretty much lied to her parents about what was going on.

Davis: What do you believe are the characteristics of an effective team member?

Matzler: Well, first, I think effective team members have to have a commitment to the team and the team agenda. Team meetings are great. We always have an agenda and we have a lot of fun. If we have discipline problems we handle them through the team. We also hold parent conferences and plan field trips when we meet. We meet daily, and I think that's important, too.

Second, I believe a sense of humor and a desire to have fun are critical for a middle school teacher. I think it is important that teachers think of ways to have fun and still maintain an academic focus. For example, we have different team rewards. I started the "BUG" award—"Bring Up Grade Award." If in the second 9 weeks a student kept every grade the same and brought at least one grade up, he or she got an award. It might be a certificate we all signed and wrote nice things on or a certificate to a favorite fast-food place. If the student did it twice, then all the teachers on our team would buy pizzas and soft drinks and bring the student to our room. It was great. We could let our hair down and tease them. We even gave pluses just so some of the straight-A students could also achieve this. The whole school did this, but on our team I know the kids really wanted this. You could see the really poor students with three Fs and a D would have only two Fs and two Ds the next time and maybe even a C the next time. They really worked for it, and we wanted to make it worthwhile. The kids loved to come and eat with the four of us. It was one thing you couldn't do individually.

Third, I believe a collegial spirit is important to the success of a team and a school. Teaching is about the best profession if a person wants to make society a little better. I never wanted to be a good teacher only for kids. I wanted to be a good teacher for other teachers, too. A lot of teachers would come and talk to me about personal things like divorces, death, and cancer. Some were good friends and some just acquaintances. It means a lot to me that people trust me. I think teachers who enter the profession should become a teacher for other teachers as well as for kids.

Davis: How does your team function and communicate from day to day?

Matzler: I am the keeper of the records. A clipboard is kept in my room so a teacher can come in, sit at my desk, and write on the clipboard. For example, we have this system at Dewey, if you "write this kid up," one copy goes to the team members, one to the assistant principal, and one to the parent. I keep all of them. I put them in a folder and about every 2 weeks I take them and staple them in chronological order. If a parent comes in we have a record. As a team, we keep extensive records. As individuals, the grade book is extremely important. When we send notes to the office, we keep a copy of them. Everything is planned in team meetings. They're the most important meetings I'm involved in because that's the heart of our team. We meet daily because we want to do things for the kids.

Davis: What do you think students like about your team?

Matzler: Having the four of us talk together when our team meets is good for them because we bring some of them into our meetings and ask for their advice and say, "This is what we're thinking. Now, what do you think?" They like giving us input.

Davis: Do the middle-level students like all the recognition that Dewey provides for them?

Matzler: They love it, and I think it is one of the most powerful tools we have in education at this level. There are so many ways for a school to recognize students I can't begin to name them all. A part of our team meetings are devoted to discussion on identifying opportunities for recognizing our students.

When kids are in writing competition, we have four teachers encouraging them. We make posters like "Way to go, Team!" for kids who win anything. We have the names of kids involved in all activities and clubs posted in a room recognizing them.

Sometimes we each take a kid and keep each other abreast of what's going on. We all compliment them and look for anything positive. If they turn in their homework, I'd say at least, "Great, you signed your name right." It's amazing how these kids come along.

In fact, I go down and beg for some of the at-risk kids to be on our team so we can work with them in a positive manner. The counselors say, "Does your team know you are doing this?" I would say, "Yes," but of course they didn't. Then I would have to go and promise them things and beg, "Oh, please, we can do something with this kid." I usually am the one who takes this kid as my project.

Davis: Are you always successful with these kids?

Matzler: Not always. For example, I'll never forget this kid named Cory. I met Cory in an in-school suspension one day. He had a very troubled background, and I asked to have him on our team. The first 9 weeks he got all Fs and a D. The D was from me. But we kept working with him, and the next 9 weeks he passed everything. And then the third 9 weeks he got all Bs and Cs, and the fourth 9 weeks he made the honor roll. He was smart, but he had a troubled family background. It was really strange. He had one sister who married a doctor and one brother who was a minister and two other brothers who were in and out of jail. He had a supportive mother, but the dad was abusive.

At the end of the year, our team gets together to give out a whole bunch of awards, like the kid with the most freckles or the craziest hairdo. But we always give an award called the "Most-Improved Eighth-Grade Student." And that year, I got to give it, and we gave it to Cory and all the kids stood up and clapped for him. They knew he deserved it. Afterward, he came in and thanked each one of us and he gave me a big hug and was crying and said, "You know, I'll never forget this year." Unfortunately, he never made it through high school; he got involved in some drugs. But the thing is, if you have four caring teachers working together, you can work miracles, and we do it every year. It's easy to convince my team to take on these challenges when they can see what's possible.

Davis: How does your team reach consensus when you don't agree on issues?

Matzler: Fortunately, we have philosophies and values very much the same. We spend a lot of time talking about issues before making decisions. We don't always agree. There are times when one or another disagrees with the other team members. But once a decision is made, we all work together to support it because there's a lot of trust between us and we also have a commitment to each other as a team.

Davis: How can teachers become good teachers who care for students?

Matzler: I think good teachers always do things for kids and I try to emulate the good teachers I've had. I've asked myself many times, "Why were these teachers good?" "Why did you want to come to their classroom?" "Why did they have good discipline?" In many of their classrooms, you could see changes in kids. Analyzing the good teachers has been important to my development as a teacher.

Davis: Do you think students really appreciate all teachers do for them at the middle school level?

Matzler: Not while they're there, but I can't begin to tell you the number of kids that come back to the middle school from the high school to say thank you. They appreciate what went on at Dewey. I'm not talking about 5 or 10, I'm talking about hundreds. It always makes us feel good when they come back.

Davis: Do you think you've ever influenced anyone to become a teacher?

Matzler: Yes, but one thing I wish we had at Dewey is a future teachers group. We tried, but there's only so many things you can do. But I do know that some kids became teachers because of the middle school teachers. All three of my kids still talk about their middle school teachers. They loved them. I think middle school teachers can make a greater influence on students than teachers at any other level.

Questions for Discussion and Activities

1. Should teachers have a written personal mission statement? What might an individual mission statement include? Write your own mission statement for your role as a middle-level educator.

2. What are some additional characteristics of team members that could be added to Ed Matzler's list?

3. Do you agree that any time you have teams there will be competition among them? Is it part of U.S. culture to be competitive? Is there such a thing as "positive competition"?

4. What was the problem with the spring fever competition? Could you suggest alternatives?

5. How often should teams meet for planning? How can team planning time be used effectively? Plan a weekly agenda for a typical core team.

6. Can administrators make a teacher's job easier? Explain.

7. What are the characteristics of at-risk kids?

8. What are some creative ways a team can reach consensus on issues when members do not function effectively because they do not share common philosophies, lifestyles, politics, values, and so forth?

9. What influence do teachers have on future teachers? Does teacher training make a difference or do we teach the way we were taught?

10. What is the current research on retention? What is the local school's policy on retention?

11. Discuss the importance of recognition in a middle school. Develop a list of categories for a recognition program in a middle school and look for kids to fit the category. Interview a group of middle school students and find something special about them that could be recognized.

Relationship to Turning Points Recommendations

- Create small communities for learning
- Ensure success for all students
- Empower teachers
- Prepare teachers for the middle level

Recommended Reading

Beane, J. A. (1993a). *A middle school curriculum: From rhetoric to reality* (2nd ed.). Columbus, OH: National Middle School Association.

Beane, J. A. (1993b). The search for a middle school curriculum. *School Administrator, 50*(3), 8-16.

Dickinson, T. (Ed.). (1992). *Readings in middle level curriculum: A continuing conversation.* Columbus, OH: National Middle School Association.

Erb, T. O., & Doda, N. M. (1989). *Team organization: Practice and possibilities.* Washington, DC: National Education Association.

Hawkins, M. L., & Graham, M. D. (1994). *Curriculum architecture: Creating a place of our own.* Columbus, OH: National Middle School Association.

Irvin, J. L. (Ed.). (1992). *Transforming middle level education: Perspectives and possibilities.* Boston: Allyn & Bacon.

Jacobs, H. (Ed.). (1989). *Interdisciplinary curriculum: Design and implementation.* Alexandria, VA: Association for Supervision and Curriculum Development.

Lipsitz, J. (1984). *Successful schools for young adolescents.* New Brunswick, NJ: Transaction Books.

Scales, P. (1992). *Windows of opportunity: Improving middle grades teacher preparation.* Chapel Hill: University of North Carolina, Center for Early Adolescence.

Scales, P. C., & McEwin, C. K. (1994). *Growing pains: The making of America's middle school teachers.* Columbus, OH: National Middle School Association.

Stevenson, C. (1992). *Teaching ten- to fourteen-year-olds.* New York: Longman.

Story 5:

Mastering the Master Schedule

Even though Dewey had been using a block-of-time schedule since the school implemented middle school practices 4 years ago, the principal, Jane Byers, knew that getting all the teams in the school to really take advantage of the flexibility in this kind of schedule would take even longer. Each year, she took time with teams to gather input about the schedule's strengths and weaknesses. She wanted them to really understand that the school's schedule should support their program and allow them to do the type of integrated curriculum that they had set as a goal. But not everyone was buying in, and Richard Hoff, the assistant principal, certainly wasn't helping. He continued to send messages to staff that ran contrary to the real meaning of a block schedule. Jane Byers knew that they had more work to do and hoped that the teachers who had visited Jefferson Middle School in Lewisville the previous week to review that school's schedule would have some new insights to share with the staff at the faculty meeting. Maybe they could help more Dewey teachers see the real beauty of the block-of-time schedule.

"If we don't really utilize the blocks of time in the schedule," thought Jane Byers, "we are really nothing more than a teamed junior high school. I hope this meeting helps more teachers see the benefits of using time in the schedule differently." She made her way to the media center for the start of the faculty meeting hoping things would go well.

Judy McKay, Mark Lyden, and Colleen Hunt were nervous about their presentation to the staff, but they knew they were well prepared for the questions and comments they anticipated from their colleagues. They had worked at Dewey long enough to know that they could expect Tim Jones to moan and groan about any new idea, and that Martha Docweiler and John Graber would add to the chorus of whiners. Because they were on three different teams, they knew they had to convince the other members of their teams to fight hard for the changes in the schedule they would be proposing at the meeting. They also knew that many of the teachers at Dewey were ready for this next step in their development, and so the trio proceeded to the media center confident that the majority at Dewey would be excited about what they had to present.

Although Jane Byers made a brief report at every faculty meeting, her practice of rotating the responsibility for the monthly faculty meetings across teams had been one of Dewey's major accomplishments. The others had resisted the idea at first but now took on their roles as facilitators of these meetings with real enthusiasm. Jane Byers was satisfied that meetings had become more productive, because time was used primarily for in-service and problem solving rather than for reporting information that could be better communicated in the weekly bulletin. She noted that teachers rarely graded papers in the back of the room during meetings any more—a major change since her first faculty meeting at Dewey 4 years ago! So today, she comfortably took a seat toward the back of the media center and smiled at the three teachers up in the front getting ready to start the meeting.

"As you know from the agenda you received in your mailbox last week, at today's meeting Mark, Colleen, and I will share what we learned about flexible uses of a block-of-time schedule from our visit to Jefferson Middle School in Lewisville last week. Then, we'll work in groups to discuss how these ideas might help us with our schedule at Dewey, we'll have a brief report from Jane, and as always, we will dismiss right on time at 4:30. Are there any questions or additions to the agenda?" asked Judy McKay.

When Tim Jones raised his hand so early in the meeting, Judy took a big gulp and hoped that trouble wasn't going to start so soon. "Yes, Tim?"

"Well, I for one don't understand why we have to have a meeting about scheduling at all. We've already got a great block schedule here at Dewey and I didn't know anyone was unhappy with it. Why do we need to change our schedule?" Martha Docweiler and John Graber nodded in agreement.

"Well," responded Judy McKay, "you may not personally want to look at scheduling changes, and I understand your reluctance to change for change's sake, but the faculty approved the school's yearly staff development plan last August and included in that plan was a study of block-of-time scheduling. So why don't we get started." The threesome distributed handouts (see Figures 2.1 and 2.2). "As you can see," Judy said, "page 1 of your handout is the current Dewey schedule and on page 2 is the Jefferson Middle School schedule."

As the staff reviewed the handouts, Judy continued, "Though it is a subtle difference, you'll notice that at Jefferson, times for each period are not indicated at the top of their schedule and they don't assign particular courses to individual teachers. They allow each team to make these decisions, so each team's block is used differently. The teachers at Jefferson said that for the most part teachers like this kind of schedule because they can decide in team meetings how to use their time."

Dewey Middle School Master Schedule

	1 8:00-8:40	2 8:42-9:22	3 9:25-10:05	4 10:05-10:45	5 10:50-11:30	6 11:33-12:17	7 12:20-12:50	8 12:55-1:35	9 1:38-2:03	10 2:05-2:45
6th	Block of Time		Unified Arts PE		Block of Time		Lunch	Block of Time		

	1 8:00-8:40	2 8:42-9:20	3 9:25-10:10	4 10:13-10:58	5 11:01-11:40	6 11:43-12:13	7 12:18-1:07	8 1:10-1:57	9 2:00-2:45
7th	Unified Arts PE		Block of Time			Lunch	Block of Time		

	1 8:00-8:45	2 8:48-9:30	3 9:33-10:18	4 10:21-11:07	5 11:10-11:40	6 11:45-12:30	7 12:33-1:20	8 1:25-2:05	9 2:05-2:45
8th	Block of Time			Lunch	Block of Time			Unified Arts PE	

Jefferson Middle School Master Schedule

20 min. Advisory Grade 6	Elective Team (96)	Instructional Team (96)	Lunch (30)	Instructional Team (144)
20 min. Advisory Grade 7	Instructional Team (144)	Elective Team (96)	Lunch (30)	Instructional Team (96)
20 min. Advisory Grade 8	Instructional Team (144)	Lunch (30)	Instructional Team (96)	Elective Team (96)

Figure 2.1. Dewey Middle School and Jefferson Middle School Schedules

"Teams can also flex their block, as they say," Mark Lyden added.

"They have developed three to five alternative schedules for their block of time, so they can quickly change their schedule depending on the activity. For example, if the team wants to get all the kids together for a movie, they can use Schedule A. This gives them 60 minutes together as a full team, then the rest of the block is broken into even periods. I think this is great because then the team doesn't have to sit down and figure out a new schedule every time they want to do something a little bit different." reported Mark. "And," he continued, "teachers at Jefferson said they even teach their kids these schedules, so if they want to change at the last minute, they just post 'Schedule A Today' on their doors and the kids know what to do."

1.	Regular Rotation
2.	1st Period Team Activity (Assembly, Team Meeting, Advisory) + Shortened Schedule Regular Rotation
3.	Same Class All Day—Weekly Rotation
4.	Alternate Rotations: Schedule A: A, E, D, C, B Schedule B: B, A, E, D, C Schedule C: C, B, A, E, D Schedule D: D, C, B, A, E Schedule E: E, D, C, B, A

Figure 2.2. Flex Your Block

Colleen Hunt heard the rumble growing from Tim Jones's corner of the room but proceeded to describe her impressions of the benefits of a flexible block schedule because most of her colleagues were listening with real interest to the presentation. "I talked to several teachers at Jefferson during our visit and asked how the teams made decisions about the use of the block time. We all know that time is critical when we have so much to cover. The Jefferson teachers said that for the most part the time each teacher needs balances out over the course of a quarter or semester, even when they use the flexible block alternative schedules. Not everyone on the team needs extra time every week, so they negotiate and trade times, knowing that if and when they need support from their teammates, they'll get it. One team said the greatest benefit of the flexible block was to give tests at the same time. If, for example, the math teacher needs to give a unit test, every teacher on the team gives the test the first 40 to 50 minutes, and then they divide the rest of their block into equal periods. I thought that sounded great."

"Several of the teams have started doing a lot more integrated units, so they don't really look at time in the same way any more," added Judy McKay. "They spend 2 or 3 days a week during their team planning time to work on curriculum now that they feel more comfortable working together and using their block differently." With that, a loud groan was heard from Martha Docweiler, who appeared to be ready to voice her concerns about "messing around with the curriculum," as she so often put it. Judy, Colleen, and Mark took this as a signal that it was time to get the staff into groups so they could discuss what they had heard before the resisters had time to unduly influence the tenor of the meeting. They quickly got the teachers into work groups of seven, making sure to mix up grade levels and teams. Each group was asked to discuss the information, list any questions members had, and determine what if any additional information members would like to have about block-of-time scheduling at the next faculty meeting.

Jane Byers noticed Richard Hoff making his way across the room to join the table where Tim Jones was already busy complaining to his group that Dewey didn't need another new schedule. After giving Judy, Colleen, and Mark a smiling nod of approval across the room, she intercepted Richard by calling him over to review the report they would make to the staff at the conclusion of the work session. She knew that more needed to be done to move the Dewey staff along and that she would have to take steps to be sure that the resisters in the school did not gain momentum and thwart the change efforts. And she had to do something about Richard Hoff!

Questions for Discussion and Activities

1. What are your impressions of the approach Jane Byers takes to staff meetings?
   a. Does research support her practice of faculty involvement?
   b. Is there any research that supports a focus on using faculty meeting time for in-service and problem solving?
   c. What problems would you anticipate from the teachers in moving in this direction?
2. What was your impression of the block-of-time schedules reviewed at the meeting?
   a. Compare and contrast the Dewey schedule to the schedule from Jefferson Middle School. What are the implications for programs in each schedule?
   b. Develop alternative options for a team's use of blocks of time. What are the implications for teaming in using alternative schedules? What are the implications for building administrators?
3. How would you handle resistant staff members?
   a. Develop a plan to address the resistance to changing the schedule represented by Tim Jones, Martha Docweiler, and John Graber's comments and behavior.

  b. Assume the role of Jane Byers. How would you work with Richard Hoff to mediate the impact of his behavior?

 4. Visit several middle schools and review their schedules.

  a. Interview staff regarding their perceptions of the use of the blocks of time and find out if teams use alternative schedules to maximize the flexibility in a block-of-time schedule.

  b. Interview building administrators to determine how schedules are developed in the school.

  c. Determine program implications of the various schedules you review.

  d. Develop a block-of-time schedule. What needs to be considered in developing a master block schedule?

Relationship to Turning Points *Recommendations*

- Create small communities for learning
- Ensure success for all students
- Empower teachers and administrators

Recommended Reading

Doda, N. (1992). Teaming: Its burdens and its blessings. In J. H. Lounsbury (Ed.), *Connecting the curriculum through interdisciplinary instruction* (pp. 45-55). Columbus, OH: National Middle School Association.

Doda, N., George, P., & McEwin, K. (1987). Ten current truths about effective schools. *Middle School Journal, 18*(3), 3-5.

Erb, T. O., & Doda, N. M. (1989). *Team organization: Promise, practices and possibilities.* Washington, DC: National Education Association.

Joyce, B., & Showers, B. (1988). *Student achievement through staff development.* New York: Longman.

Merenbloom, E. Y. (1991). *The team process: A handbook for teachers* (3rd ed.). Columbus, OH: National Middle School Association.

Oliva, P. (1993). *Supervision for today's schools* (4th ed.). New York: Longman.

Smith, W. F., & Andrews, R. L. (1989). *Instructional leadership: How principals make a difference.* Alexandria, VA: Association for Supervision and Curriculum Development.

Story 6:

Birth of the Blue Angels

Life has been crazy the last 24 hours. I think my life at school will be drastically different given the recent event. My stomach is rolling and I'm worried about what we'll do.

This feeling is familiar. It reminds me of how I felt 6 months ago when I walked for the first time through this doorway . . .

Six Months Earlier

"Hi. Is this the Blue Angels' team room? I'm looking for Jenny Mills. Is she here? Ms. Byers told me this is the eighth-grade team I've been assigned to work with this year."

As I looked around the room three pairs of eyes stared back at me. Although they appeared to welcome me with enthusiastic smiles, it was clear they were somewhat wary of me and how I would fit on the team.

Wow, was I ever nervous at that moment! It seemed that as soon as the meeting started, everyone began talking at once. It was just plain chaos for a while. As things began to settle down, I started to appraise my partners for the year.

Tim Jones has taught seventh grade science for the past 15 years. He was a resister to the middle school change a few years ago. He has adjusted to the change but was not looking forward to the move to eighth grade. Tim considers himself a traditionalist. If the wheel isn't broken, don't bother fixing it.

Bill Morris, the boys' basketball coach, has taught eighth-grade social studies for the past 5 years. The kids love his energy both on the court and in the classroom.

Jenny Mills was our chosen team leader. Jenny has taught language arts for the past 20 years. She was at the high school until Dewey Junior High became Dewey Middle School. She's a real fan of teaming and working with the kids.

I guess that leaves me, Sue Walker, to teach the math classes for the upcoming year. I'm a brand-new teacher fresh out of the university. My stomach was full of butterflies and I wanted the first day of school to be over with as soon as possible.

The first few minutes of the meeting didn't seem to be going very well, but Jenny is a take charge type of person. She had our team going in no time. She assigned duties and responsibilities and she also had us discussing team rosters and minilessons and establishing goals for the team. Because of that first meeting, it seemed we all looked to her for guidance and became dependent on her. Her leadership abilities really seemed to pull this new team through the next few weeks.

Tim, Bill, and I thought things were going great. We supported Jenny's viewpoints. We knew her expectations and we wanted to please her. But in fact, we were becoming more of a burden than an asset to the team. She needed us to cooperate, suggest, and discuss with her as peers, not to act as children hanging on her every word. Jenny needed team involvement—not team dependency.

We all knew there needed to be a change but couldn't figure out exactly what role each of us should take. Jenny was assigned as the leader but wanted to facilitate and guide us in the completion of our tasks. It was difficult for the rest of us to find a niche on our team. We did have one role filled—conflict breaker. It seemed we could always rely on Bill to find the humor in a situation to break the tension. At times, if it weren't for Bill, Jenny and Tim would have been at each other's throats.

By the end of the first quarter, we began to get used to each other's peculiarities and we started to function more as a team. We were no longer as dependent on Jenny for every move, nor were we in constant conflict with each other. We had established our roles and functions on the team. No one person assigned the specific roles, we just naturally slipped into them based on our strengths and weaknesses. It was as if the roles evolved from the process of talking and listening to each other. We not only began to develop skills to help us work as a team, but we confronted curriculum and discipline issues and instructional problems up front. No longer did we dodge a problem and pass it on to an administrator. We met the problems head on and made sure everyone was in full agreement with what we were doing. It was a nice feeling to cooperate instead of competing to complete our job.

Our students even began to notice. They started to make comments about us being a united front. There were even comments made about our team members being joined at the hip. Our lessons reflected our joint work. We even used minilinks in the classroom. The students started to make real connections between the subject matter and real-life applications.

Our motive when dealing with students was no longer to win at all costs. When we had to deal with a student on a discipline issue, we discussed the issue first, established our goals, then brought in the student. We asserted a team effort so the child and the teachers would be in a win-win situation.

Somewhere during that first semester, we became a team. We worked together, respected each other's rights and opinions, and were effective with the kids. Wow! What a first semester.

Well, that brings me up to the present day. I am really scared of going into the team meeting today. I've been comfortable in the team process for so long now that I don't know how our team will respond to the crisis at hand. Our team has come a long way. I feel we will stick together and support each other instead of breaking down and becoming four individuals working on our own agendas. The team has overcome so many obstacles in the past 6 months that we should be able to pull together and work toward a common goal for the kids. Oh, well, it's time to go in and get the team meeting started.

Jenny started the meeting by saying, "I'm sure you've heard by now that our student, John Smith, was hit by a drunk driver on his way home from school yesterday. He's in critical condition. We'll need to have a plan of action for working with our students . . ." Jenny broke down and began sobbing, and we all began to talk at once.

Questions for Discussion and Activities

1. Read George (1992) and other readings on team development.
   a. What stages do teams go through in their development?
   b. What can a team do to facilitate movement through typical development phases?
2. How will a team's dynamics impact its member's ability to develop a supportive network for each other and their students?
3. Using the characters in the story, role-play a typical team meeting. Discuss group dynamics as related to how you interact.
4. Using the characters in the story, role-play the team meeting that Jenny Mills, Bill Morris, Tim Jones, and Sue Walker will have related to the injured student.
   a. Develop a plan of action to help the students cope with having a classmate critically injured.
   b. Discuss how the injured child could pull the team apart or bring the team closer together.
5. Review several crisis plans. Design your own crisis plan for a building and a team.

Relationship to Turning Points *Recommendations*

- Create small communities for learning
- Empower teachers and administrators
- Connect schools with communities

Recommended Reading

Doda, N. (1992). Teaming: Its burdens and its blessings. In J. H. Lounsbury (Ed.), *Connecting the curriculum through interdisciplinary instruction* (pp. 45-55). Columbus, OH: National Middle School Association.

Doda, N., George, P., & McEwin, K. (1987). Ten current truths about effective schools. *Middle School Journal, 18*(3), 3-5.

Erb, T. O., & Doda, N. M. (1989). *Team organization: Practice and possibilities.* Washington, DC: National Education Association.

Lounsbury, J. H. (1992). *Connecting the curriculum through interdisciplinary instruction.* Columbus, OH: National Middle School Association.

Merenbloom, E. Y. (1991). *The team process: A handbook for teachers* (3rd ed.). Columbus, OH: National Middle School Association.

Reference

George, P. S. (1992). Four phases in the life of a team. In J. H. Lounsbury (Ed.), *Connecting the curriculum through interdisciplinary instruction* (pp. 135-142). Columbus, OH: National Middle School Association.

Story 7:

The Problem With Martha Docweiler

Sharon Becker has always been a wonderful teacher. Even nowadays, when in the faculty room you hear the kind of jealous griping common among some teachers, there is no argument that Sharon is the best teacher in the school. It is extraordinary how much she cares for children and even more remarkable how she can turn a reluctant learner with years of failure into a respectable student who in due time accepts the challenges of learning. Stories are still told how each year she requests that a particular student from an indigent home or problem background and with an extensive history of failure be placed on her team to be the team's challenge, or mission, for the year. In faculty meetings where intense issues can have the faculty split into factions, it's marvelous the way she can get to the heart of the problem, focusing on the critical issues and removing the pettiness surrounding the personalities without anyone's feelings being hurt. She speaks eloquently about the mission of education and the virtues of being a teacher. High school students frequently come back to visit her in her classroom, to say thank you and wish openly that she would come to the high school to teach. So it was a shock when the rumor leaked from the principal's office and quickly circulated throughout the school that she would not return to teach at Dewey the following school year.

Hillary Weston stood in front of Sharon's desk minutes after she heard the rumor. With her hands placed flat on the desk, she leaned forward, as if to study Sharon's face for some emotional distress. Hillary and Sharon began teaching at Dewey at the same time and remained good friends through the years. "Why didn't you let me know you were quitting?"

Sharon laughed lightly. "The fact is, I decided only yesterday."

"I know your way of deciding is to do something suddenly," Hillary said. "I know it has been a difficult year with Martha on your team."

Sharon shrugged. "A lot of things seemed to be going wrong this year."

"There are always going to be things going wrong some years."

Sharon waved her hands. She didn't want to talk about Martha Docweiler or about the problems Martha caused or anything about the school right then. She wanted to be alone. She was tired. Teaching had lost its excitement, and she wanted a different challenge.

It was when Sharon first met Martha at the opening teachers' institute day that Sharon knew all would not be well this year. Martha had been removed from her position as director of educational technology at the high school because over the previous 12 years she had successfully discouraged the use of computers and media equipment by students and faculty. Students refused to endure the verbal harassment inflicted on them each time they attempted to use the computers or video equipment. The area was commonly referred to as "Martha's Graveyard" because of the rows of computers arranged neatly like gravestones in an empty cemetery. The new high school principal immediately saw the absurd state of affairs and decided to get rid of Martha. In the end, however, it was decided, because she had tenure as a math teacher and the administration wanted to avoid dismissal proceedings, to put her back into the classroom. Because Dewey had such a strong faculty, it was suggested Martha be placed in that school with a competent and effective teacher like Sharon who would serve as a mentor and model. Sharon was asked and, to the disappointment of the other team members, agreed to accept Martha.

Martha Docweiler is a large, powerful-looking woman whose presence is noticed immediately when she enters a room. She can be pleasant when she wants to be, but more often than not, she simply criticizes people and practices she does not like or agree with. Sharon and the other team members were often willing to let Martha have her way, and if Martha had been a little less herself and a little more discerning, she could have acquired some of the qualities that had made the team she joined so popular. But Martha saw only an idealistic and sentimental team led by an emotional romanticist—which Sharon is—and determined to bring to the team the academic focus that high school teachers constantly complained was lacking at the middle school level.

From Martha's criticism, it was clear that she believed all the students on her team were underachieving: They had poor math skills and poor reading levels, produced sloppy writing, did not think critically or creatively, and in general lacked a foundation of knowledge to work with. She intended to change how things were done. She believed learning content is critical and saw her primary teaching role as a transmitter of knowledge.

The problems began immediately in August when Martha was permitted to give math placement tests to determine more effectively which students should be in algebra and which students should be in the prealgebra math class. The end result of this testing, however, was that for a period of 2 weeks, 19 student schedules were revised because of the shuffling of students from algebra to prealgebra classes. It was Ted Barrett, a counselor, who after becoming suspicious, discovered and alerted the principal that a first-period math class appeared to be loaded with mostly minority students who were academically disadvantaged and discipline problems and came from an impoverished area of the city. Confronted by this aberration from school policy and embarrassed by her stupidity in assisting Martha with tracking these students in a first-hour class so she could "deal with them all at once and get it over with first thing," Sharon and the other team members demanded that all schedules be returned to the way they originally were.

Although students are devoted to Sharon Becker, they hate Martha Docweiler and are absolutely silenced by her size and ruthlessness and ways of commanding a classroom. They are held speechless and emotionally distressed when a fellow student angers her and catches the fury of her retribution. When Eric Homer remained after class to allow Sharon to change a bandage on a blister on his foot from the basketball game the night before, he arrived a few minutes late to Martha's class with a note explaining the problem with the foot. The class had already begun the math unit test so Eric quickly took an exam from the desk and worked furiously to complete it before the end of the period because he needed to pass the test to remain eligible for the basketball team. After collecting the tests and before dismissing the class, Martha picked up a test and announced as she ripped it in halves and fourths, "This is what I do to students who come to my class late."

Overwhelmed by what this meant, Eric burst into tears as he left the room.

"You had no right to tear that boy's test up," Sharon later challenged Martha. "I was the one who kept him after to change a bandage on his foot."

"What I gave them is a lesson in punctuality," Martha responded. "Keeps them on their toes. Shows what can happen. Besides, do you think I would actually tear his test up? See, here it is. I tore up an extra copy of the test. The best way to get their attention is to use them as an example of what can happen when one gets a little too indifferent about being at the right place at the right time. Maybe if you did more of this you would have fewer discipline referrals."

It was when Martha began acting strangely at the faculty Christmas party that Sharon knew she didn't want to work with Martha any more. Martha sat on a couch by herself, sipping wine, one leg bent over the other, in her light-green pantsuit. She was telling cruel stories about people they all knew at the high school. All the stories were about high school teachers doing silly things or embarrassing themselves or just being stupid and not knowing something everybody else knew. Martha was a good mimic and it was hard not to laugh at her stories. Bill Walker laughed and Ken Wilson laughed. Ken whispered to Bill, "She must tell stories about me, too," and then he laughed at a story about John Graber, a teacher whose last name everyone thought was "Grader" because of the time he was called from his classroom by the principal who commanded him to come immediately to the office and bring his grade book. The principal needed John to defend the grade he had given a student whose irate mother and father were at that moment demanding an explanation. When John Graber showed up with a grade book void of any scores or grades, the principal was so embarrassed and angry he demanded all teachers turn in copies of their grade books every quarter from that time on. The teachers were furious at having to go through this nuisance because of his negligence. From that time on, whenever the faculty jokers were together in the faculty room and John entered, they would inevitably stand up and chant together: "Hail, Non Grader."

The problems with Martha continued. Sharon finally decided to give up and quit after Martha refused to give Latisha Ward, the team's "challenge," a passing grade for the semester. Latisha had an unfavorable family background. Her father was an alcoholic and two of her brothers were in jail. It took 3 months of nurturing and encouragement before she even spoke in anyone's class. Sharon had worked hard all semester to help Latisha keep her grades above failing, and finally the girl was beginning to make a go of it. She had passed five of her classes and needed to pass six to avoid the possibility of a retention at the end of the year. She was very close to passing in Martha's class. Martha knew the situation and when she averaged her grades, Latisha's average came out to 69.8%. She needed a 70% to pass, and Martha gave her an F, increasing the likelihood she'd be held back in eighth grade. After this, Sharon decided she didn't want to struggle with Martha any more. She had begged Martha to reconsider and give her at least a D– and a chance to graduate and go to a special program at the high school that provided incentives to people like Latisha to remain and graduate from high school. But Martha, who believed standards should not be compromised for anyone, for any reason, said, "That's reality. She will have to face it sooner or later."

Questions for Discussion and Activities

1. Why does Martha Docweiler believe being a "transmitter of knowledge" will solve the academic problems she perceives exist at Dewey? Do you agree?

2. Can different teachers ever fully work together on a team while maintaining their distinct teaching styles? Explain.
3. How important is it to match teaching styles to student learning styles?
4. What are some ways to handle Martha Docweiler?
5. Role-play the ending of the case study.

Relationship to Turning Points Recommendations

- Create small communities for learning
- Ensure success for all students
- Prepare teachers for the middle level

Recommended Reading

Ahar, J., Johnston, H., & Markle, G. (1988). The effects of teaming and other collaborative arrangements. *Middle School Journal, 19,* 22-25.

Erb, T. (1987). What team organizations can do for teachers. *Middle School Journal, 18,* 3-6.

Erb, T. O., & Doda, N. A. (1989). *Team organization: Promise, practices and possibilities.* Washington, DC: National Education Association.

Merenbloom, E. Y. (1991). *The team process in the middle school: A handbook for teachers* (2nd ed.). Columbus, OH: National Middle School Association.

Story 8:

Working With Jane Byers

Jane knew that although she had arrived at Dewey 4 years before, some of the teachers still had not fully accepted her as the principal of the school. Although they didn't come right out and say it, it seemed they were still hoping she would miss the elementary school where she had been principal before coming to Dewey and take a bid on a position when one opened in the district. Some of these same staff members had been friends with Richard Hoff for a long time and were disappointed when he was passed over and Jane Byers was hired instead for the Dewey principalship. And with all of her work to mend fences in the school, Jane knew that not everyone was on her side.

Jane characterized her style of leadership in the school as collaborative, though she would not hesitate to become autocratic if a teacher attempted to implement practices that she viewed as not being in the best interests of young adolescents. Much of the staff-development time in the school was focused on child development and learning theory so all the teachers would fully understand the physical, intellectual, social, and emotional needs of their students. As long as students' needs were the top priority, teachers had Jane's full support to try new ideas—Jane understood and accepted mistakes, false starts, and failures as part of the learning process. She wasn't afraid to roll up her sleeves and work alongside the staff in ironing out the myriad details that becoming a middle school entailed. She believed in the potential of the professionals in the building, worked tirelessly to find sources for additional funding when teachers wanted new materials, and acted as a buffer when the central office got in the way of their progress. She hoped that she was well liked by most staff in the building, but that was not her goal. Instead, she worked to earn their respect, and whether or not they always agreed, she clearly had the students' needs as her primary focus. In doing so, she knew that she might not win any popularity contests with some of the teachers.

"The situation brewing over team assignments next year could be a showdown," thought Jane. She was certain that some teachers were unhappy with her style of leadership and might make this the issue to finally get her to see the light and leave. She was also certain that other teachers had flourished since her arrival and would not hesitate to come to her defense if she needed their help. She was hopeful that a major confrontation could be avoided, but she knew also that the goal wouldn't be easy to achieve.

Jane recalled her first year as the principal of Dewey and the original process she had used for team assignments. After spending the year studying the middle school concept, the staff had voted to adopt the philosophy and to begin implementing middle school practices, including teaming, the following fall. To make interdisciplinary team assignments, Jane had developed a questionnaire for staff to complete, indicating their preferences for subject assignments and teammates. At a faculty meeting, teachers completed personality and learning styles inventories, which Jane used, along with the completed questionnaires, to make team assignments. She believed that her work with the interdisciplinary teams in the school served as a model for teachers in demonstrating how students could be teamed into cooperative groups in the classroom. So team building and team development had always been high on her list of priorities. But even with all of the careful attention she had given to team assignments, not everyone was thrilled with the outcome. Aside from the few changes that were prompted by the natural attrition in the school, teams hadn't been reorganized since that first assignment. Some teachers were anxious to be reassigned; other teams were well established and unhappy about the possibility of being reshuffled.

The last thing Jane Byers needed was an assistant principal that was working against, rather than with her, but several teachers had told her that Richard Hoff had been stirring the pot, making teachers anxious about team assignments by telling them that she had a secret plan to change all of the teams in the school for next year. Like some of the teachers, Richard hoped that this would be the issue that would send Jane packing. Though he never said anything out of line to her face, she knew that Richard did little to promote middle school philosophy and practice and that he would be happier if he were principal and Dewey was once again a traditional junior high school.

"Yes," thought Jane, "this could indeed be a showdown, and I have to be prepared."

Questions for Discussion and Activities

1. From what you have read about Jane Byers in this story and other stories in the book, how would you characterize her leadership style?

    a. Is there any research that supports her practice of collaborative decision making? What evidence do you find in the stories in the book that she shares decision making?

    b. Is there any research that supports her willingness to make autocratic decisions when she feels it necessary? What evidence do you find in the stories in the book that she has made autocratic decisions?

    c. How would you feel if you were a teacher working at Dewey?

2. Interview several building principals at the elementary, middle, and high school levels.

    a. What conclusions can you draw about the type of leadership needed at each level? What support for your conclusions do you find in the literature?

    b. What did the middle school principals you interviewed indicate was the type of leadership needed to support a middle school?

3. What are your impressions about the process used for team assignments at Dewey?

    a. Locate sample inventories that could be used with teachers to determine personality type and learning style. Complete the inventories and describe how they could be used to assist school officials in making team assignments.

    b. Locate sample questionnaires that could be used with teachers to determine subject and teammate preferences for teaming. Complete the questionnaires and describe how they could be used to assist school officials in making team assignments.

    c. Organize a debate around the question, "Should teams be reorganized next year at Dewey?" Conduct the debate. Determine a plan of action for team assignments for the coming year at the school.

Relationship to Turning Points *Recommendations*

- Create small communities for learning
- Empower teachers and administrators

Recommended Reading

Bennis, W. (1989). *Why leaders can't lead: The unconscious conspiracy continues.* San Francisco: Jossey-Bass.

Bolman, L. G., & Deal, T. E. (1991). *Reframing organizations: Artistry, choice, and leadership.* San Francisco: Jossey-Bass.

Clark, S., & Clark, D. (1994). *Restructuring the middle-level school: Implications for school leaders.* New York: State University of New York Press.

Erb, T. O., & Doda, N. M. (1989). *Team organization: Practice and possibilities.* Washington, DC: National Education Association.

George, P., Stevenson, C., Thomason, J., & Beane, J. (1992). *The middle school and beyond.* Alexandria, VA: Association for Supervision and Curriculum Development.

Designing the Middle School Curriculum

3

Story 9:

The Heart of It All

"Where has the time gone?" pondered Kristen Baker as she walked slowly to the book storage room to return her books and teacher manuals. The end of the first semester marked her last day of student teaching. "I made it!" she thought and glowed with satisfaction.

Engrossed in plans for the coming weekend, several eighth graders rounded the corner and accidentally bumped into Kristen. Apologizing, they helped her pick up her books and headed off to their morning advisory classes. Just 15 weeks ago when Kristen had first arrived at Dewey to be a student teacher with Emily Pritchart, she might have been annoyed by this group's energy and actions. Today, she is able to smile and accept their honest apology. It's not just that she feels great today, but she has come to understand middle schoolers and how they act. Her experience with the

Dewey advisory program made a strong impact on her understanding of kids and she felt lucky to have observed so many different ways to conduct advisory classes.

The only tardy bell of the day shatters the silence of the near-empty hallway. Glancing in Emily Pritchart's eighth-grade room, Kristen notices the students have already begun work on their newspaper. This advisory has undertaken the project of producing a quarterly all-school newspaper. At the last grade-level team meeting, Emily shared her feelings about all the work involved in this activity. The pride these students have developed and the teamwork they have experienced were certainly worth the time and effort on her part. Selling the newspapers has been an added reward to the students. The hardest part was getting them to decide how to spend the money. Eventually they voted to donate the funds to Ed Matzler's class.

Although Ed Matzler's advisory class is part of a different eighth-grade team, the projects they work on are for the good of the whole school. Ed's classroom is across the hall and down from Emily's but no students are present in the room. A message on the door proclaims that they are outside in front of the school if anyone needs them. With 3 weeks left before Christmas vacation, the students have used the newspaper funds and solicited donations to acquire Christmas lights to decorate the front of the school. Beautifying the grounds year round has been the goal of this advisory class. Projects have included gardening, collecting litter, and painting trash cans and bike racks. The other students are sometimes a bit jealous of the fun this group seems to have, Kristen thinks, as she remembers comments she has overheard. Then, there is Jack Caulder's science class, the next door down. Glancing at the students quietly writing in notebooks at their tables, Kristen wonders if they are doing their homework, or perhaps writing in an advisory journal, or maybe even doing a two-part activity that they will later share with each other. It's hard to tell, but silence prevails.

Kristen peeks into the next room and the students eagerly invite her in to show off their quilt. The students and their adviser, Barbara Peck, have almost completed one quilt this semester. They make Kristen guess their theme. Carefully studying the many flowers covering the blanket, she teases them by guessing, "Trees?" "Wild animals?" "How about states?" Finally, she compliments them on their excellent effort and inquires where the quilt will find a home. They have already chosen the local homeless shelter as the perfect resting place for their masterpiece. In fact, they can't wait to start on their next quilt. The new quilt will be divided into 16 equal boxes, one for each advisee and the teacher. Each square will be filled with something symbolic to the individual. What enthusiasm—even from the guys! Twelve weeks ago Kristen would never have believed that this type of project could succeed in an eighth grade. Another learning lesson to add to her extensive journal of student teaching insights!

Sandy Lasko, the special education teacher has her classroom next to the book storage room, Kristen's destination. As part of her Dewey experience, Kristen has been able to visit and participate in encore and special education class activities. Today, Sandy's students are seated in chairs in a circle. As one student tosses a koosh ball to another student, the receiving student must state a feeling and tell of a time when he or she experienced this feeling. The students are actively involved except for Greg, who is sitting sideways in his chair so no one will throw him the ball. With one foot, he kicks the chair next to him, where Ashley is sitting. Ashley is struggling to ignore him and stay with the group. Gently, Sandy removes Greg with a hug and the reassurance that it's okay to sit out today. Maybe tomorrow he'll want to join another activity. Kristen wonders how many of the other advisory teachers allow their students to opt out of an activity for the day.

She recalls leading the daily advisory class for which she was responsible as a student teacher and sometimes when she wished she had allowed a student to sit out or pass on an answer or an activity. But she always felt that she should keep all the students actively involved. Maybe the resisters could have been given an alternate activity. She'll remember this strategy when she is teaching on her own next year after graduation. She hopes it will be in a middle school with an advisory program. Though she remembers being somewhat resistant to the idea of a teacher-based guidance program at the beginning of her student teaching, she now believes that advisory is a key component of an effective school for young adolescents. The idea of having 30 minutes a day to work with 12 to 15 kids on issues that are important to their social and emotional development, without the pressure of assigning grades or giving tests as required in other classes, was at first preposterous to Kristen. But now she realizes that it was during the daily advisory period that she got to know students well and was able to build meaningful relationships with students. She doesn't want to imagine being a teacher in a school without an advisory program.

Kristen reaches her destination, turns in her books, and returns to the classroom for her last day of student teaching.

Questions for Discussion and Activities

1. Each teacher Kristen observed differed in his or her approach to advisory classes. How do you feel about this and why?
2. Which advisory activities seemed to be meeting the needs of students?
3. How might sixth-, seventh-, and eighth-grade activities differ to reflect the needs and interests of the students at these ages?
4. How do you think Kristen feels about her student teaching experience?
   a. Kristen hints that some of her advisory students may have been resisters at times. What are some strategies for resolving this problem?
   b. Should resisters be treated the same way in core classes, unified arts, special education?
5. Take the Myers-Briggs (Myers & Briggs, 1976) or the Keirsey Temperament Sorter (Keirsey & Bates, 1984). How might this knowledge impact the way you relate to adolescents and how you might approach advisory activities?

Relationship to Turning Point Recommendations

- Create small communities for learning
- Ensure success for all students
- Connect schools with communities

Recommended Reading

Ayres, K. R. (1994). Middle school advisory programs: Findings from the field. *Middle School Journal, 25*(3), 8-14.

Beane, J., & Lipka, R. (1987). *When kids come first: Enhancing self-esteem.* Columbus, OH: National Middle School Association.

Bergman, S., & Baster, J. (1983). Building a guidance program and advisory concept for early adolescents. *NASSP Bulletin, 67*(463), 49-55.

Bushnell, D., & George, P. S. (1993). Five crucial characteristics: Middle school teachers as effective advisers. *Schools in the Middle, 3*(1), 10-16.

George, P. S., & Bushnell, D. (1993). What works and why? The key to successful advisement activities. *Schools in the Middle, 3*(1), 3-9.

James, M. (1986). *Advisor/advisee: Why, what and how.* Columbus, OH: National Middle School Association.

James, M. (1993). Refocusing advisories, thematically. *Middle School Journal, 25*(1), 44-45.

National Middle School Association. (1991). *Treasure chest: A teacher advisory resource book.* Macon, GA: Panaprint.

Simmons, L., & Klarich, J. (1989). The advisory curriculum: Why and how. *NELMS Journal, 2*(2), 12-13.

Sizemore, J., & Travis, S. (1986). Teacher based guidance. *Dissemination Services on Middle Grades, 17*(8), 1-6.

Stewart, W. J. (1993). Optimizing classroom guidance. *Middle School Journal, 25*(1), 41-43.

References

Keirsey, D., & Bates, M. (1984). *Please understand me: Character and temperament types.* Del Mar, CA: Prometheus Nemesis.

Myers, I. B., & Briggs, K. C. (1976). *Myers-Briggs type indicator* (reprint). Palo Alto, CA: Consulting Psychologists Press.

Story 10:

You Mean I Have to Give Up Content?

The tension at team meetings had been growing for a long time. Even in Purple Paradise's five-person team, battle lines had been drawn. The old arguments of process versus product, discovering versus covering the curriculum, student-centered versus teacher-centered classrooms accounted for most of the voiced discussions and even more of the awkward silences in the team room.

As Emily Pritchart looked around at the room waiting for her fellow team members to arrive, the weariness and apprehension she felt almost convinced her not to begin another discussion—or more likely, an argument—about their upcoming interdisciplinary unit (IDU). After all, it seemed hypocritical to spend time planning a big, flashy IDU when so little curriculum integration had taken place so far this year. The team had had major battles just agreeing to sequence some of their "sacred" units, let alone actually integrating content or team teaching or, heaven forbid, sacrificing some of their traditional curriculum to the "god of integration."

As a language arts teacher, the benefits were so clear to Emily. Language arts—reading, writing, speaking, and listening—were tools, tools that could and should be used to learn all things. Skills in these areas were best developed through use and the more authentic and purposeful the use the better. The science and math folks, especially, saw things very different-ly. They wanted to protect their content, they wanted students to practice discreet skills, and they defended a rigid sequencing of lessons and units. In other words, they saw any integration as an encroachment on their turf. And IDUs? These were a total abandonment of discipline, considered in the best light as playtime and in the worst as anarchy.

In all fairness though, Emily could see some of Jack Caulder's arguments. Good science instruction, he insisted, is more than teaching a bunch of isolated facts. For students to truly learn science they must become scientists. (Hadn't she said the same thing about her students becoming writers?) They must practice and learn to appropriately apply the science process skills of observing, measuring, and hypothesizing. He insisted that he had yet to see an interdisciplinary unit that contained any real science. Reading or writing about scientists during a Renaissance theme didn't count as real science, nor did graphing favorite bubblegum flavors count as real math.

Thus the rub—how to integrate curriculum, use best-practice middle school teaching strategies, and maintain the integrity of each discipline. It shouldn't be that difficult, Emily thought. My job is clear. I need to challenge my team to think differently about the work we do. Easier said than done. Our training, the structure of our school, and the materials we use (including those damnable district curriculum guides) all combine to reinforce a discipline-based and compartmentalized view of the world.

If we want our students to see the interconnections that bring meaning, relevance, and energy to learning, we have to move off dead center to reconsider our beliefs and review our practice. Integrating curriculum is a real-world approach to learning. That should appeal to my pragmatists. They can't deny that it increases student motivation and interaction, but how can I convince them that they will not be sacrificing the basics of their discipline?

Questions for Discussion and Activities

1. Compose definitions for interdisciplinary unit and integrated curriculum that point out how these are different and related.
2. Create a list of reasons for and against interdisciplinary study from several points of view.
3. Brainstorm a list of institutional inhibitors to integrating curriculum in a middle school.
4. How does interdisciplinary teaching and integrated curriculum support other school improvement plans?
5. Why did it seem hypocritical to Emily Pritchart to be "planning a big, flashy IDU when so little curriculum integration had taken place so far this year"?
6. Role-play the upcoming team planning meeting. How might Emily Pritchart approach her team members? What is their likely response? Try to come to an agreement on an interdisciplinary unit that all of the team members can agree on.

Relationship to Turning Points Recommendations

- Teaching a core of common knowledge
- Ensuring success for all students
- Empowering teachers and administrators

Recommended Reading

Beane, J. (1993). *A middle school curriculum: From rhetoric to reality* (2nd ed). Columbus, OH: National Middle School Association.

Beane, J. (1993). The search for a middle school curriculum. *School Administrator, 50*(3), 8-16.

Dickinson, T. (Ed.). (1992). *Readings in middle level curriculum: A continuing conversation.* Columbus, OH: National Middle School Association.

Jacobs, H. (Ed.). (1989). *Interdisciplinary curriculum: Design and implementation.* Alexandria, VA: Association for Supervision and Curriculum Development.

Lounsbury, J. H. (Ed.). (1992). *Connecting the curriculum through interdisciplinary instruction.* Columbus, OH: National Middle School Association.

Stevenson, C., & Carr, J. F. (1993). *Integrated studies in the middle grades: Dancing through the walls.* New York: Teachers College Press.

Vars, G. (1987). *Interdisciplinary teaching in the middle grades: Why and how.* Columbus, OH: National Middle School Association.

Story 11:

The Dewey Middle School Menu

Jane Byers and her staff have been working hard on next year's schedule. She has sponsored in-service workshops, working faculty meetings, breakout sessions, and group discussions. Everything seemed to be going very well. The staff was starting to understand the need for block-of-time scheduling and how to use it more efficiently. Most of the core teams had even begun talking about setting up preexisting flexible schedules. Then the students could have little schedule charts in their agendas to refer to when there was a change in the daily pattern of events. But there was an undercurrent of discontent beginning to be heard from parts of the faculty.

In the faculty lounge, there were rumblings and grumblings from a group of teachers who felt their concerns were not even being considered in the scheduling procedure. Their belief was that scheduling was done for the convenience of the so-called academic part of the curriculum and consideration was not given to the other vital parts of the current educational program. The majority of the faculty could not understand that feeling. In fact, most of the faculty felt Jane Byers was going overboard in trying to include them in the scheduling. Some of the teachers who were upset were from the encore team, the unified arts area of the curriculum.

It had finally gotten to the point where Jim Johnson, the industrial arts teacher, was ready to blow. He felt if one more core teacher spoke to him about the great advantages that block-of-time scheduling provided for both the students and teachers, he might do something he would regret later. He didn't want to feel that way about colleagues, but he felt his personal needs were being overlooked. He supported the middle school philosophy but felt little research had been completed on how to include his discipline more fully into the program.

Among themselves, the unified arts teachers have been complaining. Their feelings went from "We've always been treated this way" to "I can't take it anymore." Two of the nontenured teachers, however, felt they should keep quiet. They didn't want to bring any unnecessary attention to themselves. And they didn't want to be seen as negative.

As a group, the unified arts teachers felt the administration viewed the encore curriculum as just that—*encore,* not the core academic courses. Their courses were not the emphasis of the curriculum, so all their efforts were to be supplementary to the rest of the school's program.

The core teachers indirectly displayed the "unimportant" attitude. They would never say it out loud to a colleague, of course, but their values and norms were expressed in their actions. Although not all the teachers felt this way, a small group, rooted in old departmental paradigms, bred an atmosphere of competitiveness typical of the old junior high school culture.

At times, it even seemed as of the students similarly denigrated unified arts courses. It was not uncommon to hear students make remarks such as, "Do we get a grade for this class?" and "Does this count for anything?" When this attitude was conveyed by students, encore teachers found it almost unbearable. Some students felt they were only "in school" when they were in their core classes. The emphasis on core curriculum from the national to the local board levels seemed to encourage this attitude. Students behaved differently when they felt they were not held accountable.

Jim Johnson finally decided he needed to take his team's concerns to the principal. He had worked with Jane Byers before on a number of projects, so he felt she would at least be objective about the situation.

Johnson: Ms. Byers, do you have some time to listen to a few of my team's concerns?

Byers: Come on in, Jim. I have time to discuss any concerns you have. I know this winter has been hectic trying to get everything ready for next year's schedule. What's on your mind?

Johnson: I really don't know where to start. I'm sure you have heard the rumors floating around the school about the unified arts team. We are feeling a little left out of the system.

Jane Byers nodded, recognizing that Jim Johnson was feeling real anguish over this issue. She had already heard rumors of dissatisfaction from the encore team. As she put together all the knowledge she had on the problem, she realized there was a real dilemma brewing at Dewey.

Byers: Jim, this is what I hear you telling me. Your team feels you are not a part of the educational process here at Dewey.

Johnson: That's right. We have the feeling we are the supplementary curriculum, that our curriculum isn't, for some reason, as important as the "core" studies. And it isn't just with the scheduling of classes for next year. It is with the values displayed by you, the faculty, the students, and some of their parents.

Byers: Wow, Jim. I didn't realize I displayed the attitude of not valuing your classes. This has come as a real surprise to me.

Johnson: Don't get me wrong, we like working with you on projects, but at times we feel slighted.

Byers: Jim, let me recap what I think I heard. The mass feeling from the encore team is a feeling of being a supplementary program. You feel that the school and community do not value the worth of your programs.

Johnson: That seems to cover the main issue.

Byers: What other issues are on your mind?

Johnson: That covered the most important feeling, but additional problems fall into this scene. I realize the core teams meet during our class time, but some of the teams do not give us the courtesy of deciding when to pull a child from our classes. A sense of professional courtesy is not displayed. They just come down and state they need to see so-and-so. There is no communication of why, may I see, would it be all right if I spoke with, or allowing me to say the child is busy now.

Byers: Are you saying that the core teams take advantage of your instructional time?

Johnson: Yes, at times I feel that way. I agree with having the teams deal with discipline problems and achievement issues with the child. I have seen how our major behavioral problems have decreased through the middle school concept. I just would like to be treated as a professional! Give me notice prior to pulling a child. Twenty-four hours would be great! I could make adjustments for the child's assignments in my class. Or if I am giving a test, maybe we could work out a different solution.

Byers: You feel you are not always treated as a professional by the way teams pull students from your class?

Johnson: Yes.

Byers: Are there any other items you would like to discuss?

Johnson: Well, there is one more issue. The teams are really busy working on integrating their curriculums. We, as a team, would like to be a part of that development. We know that our curriculum provides the application for many theories presented in their courses. If they would ask us, we would be glad to help them plan. It would even help to make our educational program here at Dewey a complete program, not a fragmented program.

Byers: That's a really good insight into the curriculum issues here. We are working hard to develop interdisciplinary units. It only makes sense to include, not exclude, the unified arts division of the program.

Johnson: Well, thanks for listening. I really needed to release some of the stress I've been feeling.

Byers: It seems to me that we just began to pick out the real issues here. I believe there are many more items we need to discuss. Let's set a time to meet so we can pick apart a few of these problems and develop a plan to help overcome the feelings of dissatisfaction on your team.

Questions for Discussion and Activities

1. List the important issues in the case. Explain why there was concern among the encore, or unified arts team, about each of the issues.
2. Why would nontenured teachers be less likely to express their concerns? What are some ways the faculty and administration could help the new teachers feel more secure in expressing their feelings?
3. How could Jane Byers convince the unified arts team that she values their contribution to the educational program at Dewey?
4. Develop an interdisciplinary unit that includes at least two of the unified art disciplines.

Relationship to Turning Points Recommendations

- Create small communities for learning
- Teach a core academic program
- Ensure success for all students
- Empower teachers and administrators
- Improve academic performance through better health and fitness

Recommended Reading

Beane, J. (1993). *A middle school curriculum: From rhetoric to reality* (2nd ed.). Columbus, OH: National Middle School Association.

Beane, J. (1993). The search for a middle school curriculum. *School Administrator, 50*(3), 8-16.

Bergman, S. (1992). Exploratory programs in the middle level school: A responsive idea. In J. Irvin (Ed.), *Transforming middle level education* (pp. 179-192). Boston: Allyn & Bacon.

Compton, M., & Hawn, H. (1993). *Exploration: The total curriculum.* Columbus, OH: National Middle School Association.

Toepfer, C. (1992). Middle level school curriculum: Defining the elusive. In J. Irvin (Ed.), *Transforming middle level education: Perspectives and possibilities* (pp. 205-243). Boston: Allyn & Bacon.

Story 12:

The Team That
Tried Inclusion

Some of the teachers at Dewey Middle School are not happy campers. They feel that inclusion of special education students into their classrooms has been thrust upon them without any real plan or consideration for the effect on teachers and students. When these teachers' discontent became evident, Richard Hoff invited all involved to meet in the media center after school to discuss their perceived problems.

At first, the teachers who assembled in the media center were somewhat reluctant to say anything. Perhaps they felt being proinclusion was politically correct and any negative sentiments might be perceived as unsupportive of students with disabilities. After some dancing around the issue by Richard Hoff, Tim Jones took a deep breath and said, "I don't think it's right to expect us to create special lessons or give special treatment for the special education kids who come to our classes. If they are in our class, then—well—they should be treated just like the rest of the students."

Tim Jones's opinion brought some nods of agreement and a murmuring throughout the group. And then a rush of ideas and opinions were blurted out:

"We have never been trained to work with these kids."

"They need to come to class prepared to meet my standards and goals."

"I treat them all the same—nothing special."

"The classroom should reflect the real world."

"Singling them out has negative consequences, I think."

"I want to help these kids, I really do, but I don't know what I'm supposed to do with them."

"I don't mind having the ones that are a little slow and those LD kind, but honestly, are we expected to include those poor children from Sandy Lasko's class? And what about those emotionally disturbed kids in the portable building? Are they going to come into my classroom and wreak havoc?"

There was a pause in the murmuring and what seemed like a long silence followed. Finally, Connie Jackson spoke, "Our team has been dealing with these issues all year. I think we unofficially consider ourselves the seventh-grade inclusion team. That's not to say that the other teams aren't doing inclusion, but we have really worked with Priscilla Mac and have implemented lots of modifications and planned alternative assignments to accommodate our special learners. It has really helped those kids who seem to fall through the cracks. Priscilla Mac joins us during our planning time on a regular basis. In fact, I think we consider her part of our planning team, although the kids in her special classroom span all grade levels."

Priscilla Mac spoke up: "Yes, Connie and the rest of her team have been extremely cooperative with the special education department, and we've had some real success stories. They use cooperative learning and plan group activities so that everyone in their classes has an opportunity not only to be successful but also to be a group leader at one time or another. Every team member has been to a workshop on strategies for inclusion. Their excitement about what they have learned is truly contagious. I have really enjoyed working within a team format. Although the special education teachers meet periodically, we don't work as a unit."

Priscilla Mac paused and scanned the faces in the room. She obviously had more to say but was hesitant. Finally, she continued, choosing her words very carefully. "I am very impressed with what this team has done to help learners who have difficulty succeeding." She cleared her throat. "But I have some real concern about our so-called inclusion efforts. To be honest with you, I don't think what we are doing at Dewey is really inclusion. Students from my classroom are being mainstreamed into academic classes more than ever before, but they are not being included." Again she paused, uncertain if she should risk stepping over this line. "There is a difference between inclusion and mainstreaming. . . . It may be a subtle difference, but there is a difference."

Richard Hoff, who had been listening to the teachers vent their feelings, said, "We do have a great deal more kids included in the academic classes, and students from Sandy Lasko's class are going to lunch with the other students. They have participated in some physical education activities, and they have—"

Priscilla Mac interrupted, "Yes, Richard, I am quite aware of what is being done. I am also aware of the attitude with which it is done."

"Excuse me, Priscilla," Richard Hoff said, "but I think your kids and Sandy's behaviorally disordered students are treated very well."

"That's just what I'm talking about!" Priscilla Mac answered. "Did you hear yourself? You spoke of my kids and Sandy's students. There is no real sense of belonging in the school community for these kids. The students who come to my classroom for part of the day are viewed as belonging to me, even if they are in general education classes for the majority of the school day. Ultimately, they are my students, not Ken Wilson's, not Nicole Chipperd's, not Dewey Middle School students."

She had more to say. "I'm not talking about how they are treated. I'm talking about how decisions are made about the amount and what kind of so-called inclusion is tolerated. In a truly inclusive school community, there is no acceptance standard. Everybody belongs. You don't have to have a ticket to get in. The prevailing attitude here is that certain standards have to be met before they are allowed in. They are 'mainstreamed' in because they meet the minimum standards or as an act of kindness.

"Not all of those kids in Sandy's class live in this neighborhood, but some of them do. Not all of the students with severe disabilities in the portable buildings live in this neighborhood, but some of them do. But all of them go to Dewey Middle School. They are all part of this school community. Some of the kids in Sandy's class are the same age as sixth graders; some are seventh- and some are eighth-grade age. It's the same with the kids in the portable buildings, but they never get called sixth graders or seventh graders or eighth graders. Have you ever really listened to the announcements calling the students to an assembly? The sixth graders get called first. Then the seventh and then the eighth graders get called. Then there is an announcement for Priscilla's and Margene's resource classes to come. Sandy's class never gets called. Do you want to know how they handle the students in the portable building? If someone remembers, Liz Rogers receives a note that there will be an assembly. She may take her class when Priscilla's and Sandy's classes are called if she thinks her students can handle it."

Connie Jackson looked at the teachers in the media center, again very confidently, and stated, "As I said before, our team is very conscientious about inclusion. We have tried all the strategies that have been recommended. I suppose if we have to we can even include kids from Sandy's room. We don't have any problem with letting them come in. I'm sure that with some thought we can even work in some of those students in the portable building. Our team has tried inclusion and we are very pleased with what has happened. We will be glad to share our ideas with other teams."

"Thank you, Connie," said Richard Hoff. "This has been very enlightening. This discussion has certainly given me a lot to think about."

Questions for Discussion and Activities

1. Discuss the following as a large group or in cooperative groups:

     a. Are there hidden barriers that segregate individuals with disabilities?

     b. How does the attitudinal segregation of individuals with disabilities mirror other types of segregation?

2. As a large group or in cooperative groups, brainstorm ways to include students with special needs in the school community other than through placement in general education classrooms.

3. Hold an audience participation debate on the topic, "All learners should be in general education classrooms with their age peers."

4. Discuss the following challenges:

     a. How can you change your curriculum to better fit individual needs?

     b. How would you re-create your school community to be more inclusive of all students and personnel?

5. Visit middle schools with special education teachers as part of a general education team, with special education more separate, and with full inclusion. Interview the staff. Determine which model you feel is more effective and why.

Relationship to Turning Points *Recommendations*

- Create small communities for learning
- Ensure success for all students

Recommended Reading

Cuban, L. (1989). The "at-risk" label and the problem of urban school reform. *Phi Delta Kappan, 70,* 780-784, 799-801.

Ferguson, D., Ferguson, P., & Bogdan, R. (1987). If mainstreaming is the answer, what is the question? In V. Richardson-Koehler (Ed.), *Educators' handbook: A research perspective* (pp. 394-419). New York: Longman.

George, P., & Alexander, W. (1993). *The exemplary middle school.* New York: Harcourt Brace Jovanovich.

Hanline, M., & Murray, C. (1984). Integrating severely handicapped children into regular public schools. *Phi Delta Kappan, 66,* 273-276.

Story 13:

Learning Outside the Classroom Walls

Nicole Chipperd walked toward the lounge, her mind filled with thoughts about her team's service-learning project: "It's the Christmas season and all of us in the seventh grade have adopted the local nursing home for our Christmas project. The students have been planning for the month of December all year long. They have been earning money through bake sales and magazine sales. The money they have earned goes toward presents for the patients at the nursing home. In choir, Carl Butler, and Cindy Lopez in band have been preparing the students for the concert they will perform for the residents. Gretchen Lipson in art has been helping the students make ornaments for the tree and the hallways at the nursing home. It is so great to see all of the students and teachers working together to make this project a success."

Meanwhile, in front of Nicole Chipperd's room, Betty and Sandy, two seventh graders involved in the project, talked about the upcoming event.

"I'm so excited for the concert tomorrow," Betty exclaimed. "We have worked so hard, but it is all worth it because the residents just love all that we have done for them. The little ornaments and the visits seem to make them so happy. This whole project has been wonderful!"

"I know, they get so happy about everything we do," Sandy said. "I bet they are going to go nuts when we give them their presents. I have grown very attached to them. It's like having a whole bunch of grandparents. I'm going to be sad when this is all over."

Nicole Chipperd overheard the last part of the conversation between Betty and Sandy as she approached her room. She told them, "You know, you can go visit them on your own once the project is over. You don't just have to go with the school."

"Yeah, I know," Sandy answered. "But it would be weird to go by myself. I like going with the group. Maybe we can continue the project all year?"

"I'm not sure about that, but it is a wonderful idea. It seems like everyone involved has gotten so much out of the project. Maybe I will bring it up with Ms. Byers," Nicole Chipperd replied.

At the other end of the seventh-grade hallway, another group of seventh graders were not as fond of the project as everybody else seemed to be.

"I will be so glad when this project is over. I am tired of going to the nursing home, and I don't want to spend my Friday night singing and handing out presents to those old people. Why doesn't their own family bring them presents?" Luke asked.

"I don't know. It should not be our job to entertain those old folks. I can't wait until this stupid thing is over," Mike said.

"If we had to spend an entire semester working on some project, why couldn't it have been something better than adopting a stupid nursing home?" Roger added.

Just as Mike was about to answer, Jane Byers walked up behind them. She had heard most of the conversation and was not very happy with the boys.

"Luke, Mike, and Roger, I am very disappointed with what I just heard," she told them. "Your service project is very important. You have made this Christmas very special for the residents of Oakdale Manor. The residents normally don't receive many presents and they never get a private music concert. This project was meant as a way for your class to appreciate and learn from the older population in our community and for them to meet and appreciate the younger generation in the community. It was hoped that both groups could learn something from this project. Do you understand why this is so important?"

"Yes, we understand, and we will try to enjoy the concert," Luke replied.

"Good. I will be looking forward to hearing all of your lovely voices at the concert tomorrow. Now, you had better get off to class." Jane Byers said as she turned back toward her office.

"Yeah, right, like we are really going to enjoy ourselves. Who does she think she's kidding? There is no way I am going to sing tomorrow. I'll move my lips like this," Roger said as he portrayed his most energetic lip-synch posture.

The boys continued to complain about the project the entire way to class. They just didn't understand the meaning of the project. Meanwhile, Jane Byers also pondered her exchange with the students. "Did I get through to them? Do they understand that service learning is so important to our students and our community? We need to come up with better ways to make everyone understand how meaningful it could be." She knew she'd need to promote discussion in the school to clarify a shared vision and expectations for service learning.

Questions for Discussion and Activities

1. Why is service learning important for the students and the community? Find articles in the literature that support the integration of service learning into the middle grades curriculum.
2. How could Jane Byers have handled her conversation with the students differently? Are there more effective ways of handling student resistance?
3. Generate a list of other service-learning projects appropriate for the middle grades.
4. Contact various schools in your area to identify what, if any, service learning occurs in the school. Interview teachers, students, and administrators to identify effective strategies for developing meaningful service-learning projects that impact students, staff, and community in positive ways.
5. What, if any, service learning are you engaged in as part of your own professional development? Is service learning appropriate only for students in schools?

Relationship to Turning Points Recommendations

- Ensure success for all students
- Prepare teachers for the middle level
- Connect schools with communities

Recommended Reading

Clark, S., & Clark, D. (1994). *Restructuring the middle level school: Implications for school leaders.* New York: State University of New York Press.

George, P., & Alexander, W. (1993). *The exemplary middle school.* New York: Harcourt Brace Jovanovich.

Wiles, J., & Bondi, J. (1993). *The essential middle school.* New York: Macmillan.

Teaching and Learning in Middle School

4

Story 14:

But Jason Just Won't Cooperate

All sixth and seventh graders at Dewey were privileged to have Jim Johnson for their industrial arts teacher. Students were never disappointed with the new projects he continually devised—no repeated activities in shop class! His philosophy was "Change is exciting—redundancy is a waste of time."

Jim Johnson thrived on challenges and he was usually successful at inspiring his students to use critical thinking skills to help them solve the problems he presented to them. Knowing that the shop class environment was foreign to many of the girls as well as to some boys, he presented his lessons carefully and thoroughly so that all students would feel prepared for the projects. He even *required* students to pose questions to the teacher or other students as part of the lesson. "The only bad question is the one not asked!" posted on the bulletin board clearly communicated his philosophy.

The year before, Jim Johnson had attended an all-day staff development workshop on cooperative learning techniques. "Ah has" kept popping in his brain as the day progressed. Grouping students to work together was a method he had previously used in his classroom, but these new structured guidelines were precisely what he needed for greater effectiveness, and thereafter, as he developed his lesson plans, he incorporated cooperative activities as often as possible. His main objective was to improve student achievement via collaboration. His other goal was to help students increase their social skills. Some of the advantages he noticed when he used cooperative strategies were that most of the students stayed involved throughout the activity. They supported one another, solved problems as a team, had higher achievement levels, and seemed to retain the material longer.

Jim Johnson's success with cooperative teaming was widely known. But he had met his match with Jason! Belligerent, intolerable, selfish, and defiant were all adjectives used to describe this tow-headed, freckled-faced seventh grader. Just prior to Jason's 12-week industrial arts class, the counselor Ted Barrett contacted Jim Johnson. Jason had recently entered into a positive behavior contract with the counselor, and Ted wanted Jim to know about the pact also.

Some days were better than others for Jason and the class. "Sharing pair" activities were often a disaster because of Jason's bossy nature. Either he tried to overpower his partner or he clammed up and refused to help. But Jim never gave up on Jason. Just prior to a cooperative learning group activity, Jim took some steps to try to ensure success for the group. First, he handpicked Jason's teammates. Next, he met with each one individually to praise them for possessing patience and tolerance and to let them know that these qualities just might be challenged while working with Jason.

The final group activity for their industrial arts rotation did generate a great deal of excitement among the students. The challenge was to see which team's bridge could withhold the heaviest weight. Each team had equal supplies to work with, minimum standards to meet, and prior lesson knowledge of basic physics and structural support systems. Jason's team immediately set to work on the task at hand. Jim Johnson's role as overseer allowed him to rove the room to facilitate and monitor each group's process. In fact, one rule was that an individual student could not approach the teacher with a question or problem. Any situation had to be addressed to the group first and only if the group as a whole could not remedy the problem could the teacher be confronted. Conferring with the teacher as a first-line strategy was discouraged.

The second day into the project, as plans were being drawn, Jason started to show signs of resistance. Try as they might, his teammates found it difficult to keep him actively involved. At one point, Sue signaled to Jim Johnson, who made his presence available to the group. After quietly observing Jason's behavior, Jim requested that Jason run an errand for him and deliver a message to the office. With Jason gone, Jim gave the group an encouraging pep talk and planning resumed.

On the third day, Jason was absent. The team members marveled at how much they accomplished and how relaxed they were without Jason. They completed the final blueprints for their bridge and were ready to start building it the next day. They were flushed with confidence as they locked up their design, smug in the knowledge that they were the first to finish this stage.

Jason came in tardy to class on the fourth day. The expression on his face and his clenched fists clearly indicated his mood. Joining his group, he was dismayed to discover that the bridge plans had been finalized without him. He loudly reproached his group for not awaiting his input. He wanted to start all over again.

With only one and one-half class periods left to build the structure, his teammates tried to convince Jason that they should move ahead and concentrate on making the sturdiest bridge ever built. But Jason was angry. He fumed, pouted, and stomped away to sit near the sink. Jim Johnson suspected that Jason's mood was the result of problems he brought with him to class that day. He attempted to talk with Jason, but Jason only withdrew further.

As Jason refused to work with his group, Jim suggested an alternative task. Jason just wanted to be left alone. Through glowering eyes, he watched his group as they set about securing their popsicle sticks and toothpicks in place. Just as the class was ending, Jason jumped off his stool, ran over to his team's worktable, and destroyed the partially completed bridge with one karate chop.

Silence, then disbelief, followed the violent display. Jim Johnson dismissed the class and then walked with Jason to the counselor's office.

Questions for Discussion and Activities

1. What is your impression of Jim Johnson as an instructor?
   a. Do you feel that a one-day workshop qualified him to use cooperative learning group activities in his class?

    b. Should Jim Johnson have talked with Jason's teammates prior to starting the project? What effect, if any, did this have on the project's outcome?

    c. Jason was allowed to sit out from the group. Is this an acceptable alternative for group work? If not, in what other ways could this situation be handled?

2. What relationship exists between the counselor Ted Barrett and Jim Johnson?

    a. Do you feel that Ted Barrett performed the role of a disciplinarian at Dewey by working with Jason on a behavior contract? Should a school counselor play a role in discipline?

    b. What might a *positive behavioral contract* include?

    c. Why did Jim Johnson take Jason to the counselor after dismissing the class?

3. What are some possible causes for Jason's behavior?

    a. Jason's reputation seemed to precede him. How do labels influence students' behavior?

    b. How can Jim Johnson help Jason gain acceptance by the class?

    c. Should Jason be forced to work in a group setting if he resists? What are the possible outcomes?

4. What are the advantages and disadvantages of randomly selecting students in cooperative learning groups?

    a. Jim preselected his classroom group. Is this an acceptable practice? Why or why not?

    b. Should "academically gifted" students be isolated on separate teams together? Why or why not?

    c. Review the literature on cooperative learning to support your responses.

5. Visit several classrooms in which cooperative learning is used as a teaching strategy. Discuss your observations in light of the roles of the teacher and student in traditional and cooperative classroom settings.

Relationship to Turning Points *Recommendations*

- Ensure success for all students
- Prepare teachers for the middle level

Recommended Reading

Bellanca, J. (1992). *The cooperative think tank II: Graphic organizers to teach thinking in the cooperative classroom.* Palatine, IL: Skylight.

Bellanca, J. A., & Fogarty, R. (1991). *Blueprints for thinking in the cooperative classroom.* Palatine, IL: Skylight.

Clarke, J., Wideman, R., & Eadie, S. J. (1990). *Together we learn.* Scarborough, Ontario: Prentice Hall Canada.

Coleman, M. R. (1993). *Cooperative learning and gifted students: Report on five case studies.* Chapel Hill: North Carolina University, Gifted Education Policy Studies Program.

Evans, P. (1993). Cooperative learning: Passing fad or long-term promise? *Middle School Journal, 24*(3), 3-7.

Gartin, B. C. (1993). Staff development on cooperative learning strategies: Concerns and solutions. *Middle School Journal, 24*(3), 8-14.

Janssen-O'Leary, S. C. (1994). Interdisciplinary teaching and cooperative learning: A perfect combination for the middle school. *Social Science Record, 31*(1), 28-33.

Johnson, D. W., & Johnson, R. T. (1987). *Learning together and alone: Cooperative, competitive, and individualistic learning* (2nd ed.). Englewood Cliffs, NJ: Prentice Hall.

Klemp, R. M. (1993) Cooperative literacy in the middle school: An example of a learning-strategy based approach. *Middle School Journal, 24*(3), 19-27.

Richards, P. M. (1993). A step beyond cooperative learning. *Middle School Journal, 24*(3), 28-29.

Ruest, L. D. (1994). Learning through collaboration: A middle school example. *Social Science Record, 31*(1), 34-37.

Shlomo, S. (Ed.). (1994). *Handbook of cooperative learning methods.* Westport, CT: Greenwood.

Slavin, R. E. (1991). *Student team learning: A practical guide to cooperative learning* (3rd ed.). Washington, DC: NEA Professional Library.

Story 15:

What About Standardized Tests?

Green: Hello, Ms. Holiday. I'm Ms. Green, Mary Ann's math teacher.

Holiday: Hello, Ms. Green. I'm here because I'm very confused about the progress Mary Ann is making. At the beginning of the school year, we got test scores on a computerized printout. Mary Ann has brought her report card home two times, and she has brought home a notebook with some of her work—a portfolio she called it.

Green: Ms. Holiday, there is no need to be concerned about Mary Ann's progress. I believe she is doing fine.

Holiday: Fine! What does that mean? I remember on the computer print-out she had 98 percentile and 12th grade by math computation. But on her last report card, she got a C in math. On her work she brought home, there were all kinds of notes. One said Mary Ann has learned algebraic equations. That sounds pretty good, but when I see C for math, I think that learning algebraic equations must not be good enough. Because her test scores were so high, it seems like she should be getting As in math. Has she been playing around in class?

Green: Mary Ann is a well-behaved student. The test scores you received at the beginning of the year were from a standardized test that was given at the end of last year. Standardized tests are nationally normed. That means that the publishing company that develops the test asks students all across the country to take the test. They try to make sure the group of students reflect the population of U.S. schools. For example, if 8% of students nationwide are African American, then, 8% of the students tested in the norming group should be African American. The scores of the normed test group become the standard to which other students are compared. Therefore, Mary Ann's test scores reflect her achievement compared to other students who took the same test. Compared to other students her age, her achievement in math, based on that particular test, is outstanding.

Holiday: That's great, but can you explain why she made a C in math if her achievement is so great?

Green: Well, for one thing, the standardized tests may not match our curriculum exactly. Standardized tests are usually multiple choice with some paper-and-pencil computation, and the questions go from easy to hard. Mary Ann answered enough questions correctly to give her a high score compared to her grade peers. But our expectations for students at Dewey go beyond answering multiple choice questions and computation. During the last grading period, we put a lot of emphasis on problem solving. Part of the problem-solving process is to demonstrate how to arrive at a solution more than one way. If I recall correctly, Mary Ann has good computation skills, but she does have a little difficulty looking at a problem more than one way.

Holiday: So, what do I need to pay attention to—the standardized test scores, her report card, or her portfolio? I just want to make sure Mary Ann will be ready for high school and college.

Green: You don't have to worry, Ms. Holiday. Mary Ann is doing fine.

Ms. Holiday left the conference, but she didn't look satisfied. Leslie Green didn't feel satisfied, either. She kept thinking about what Ms. Holiday said—"So, what do I pay attention to—the standardized test scores, her report card, or her portfolio?" Jane Byers walked by the conference room and noticed Leslie Green sitting there.

Byers: How did your conference with Ms. Holiday go?

Green: Okay, I guess. [Pauses] No, it really didn't go okay. Ms. Holiday asked a legitimate question, and I didn't give her a straight answer. [Jane Byers looked puzzled, and Leslie Green recounted her conversation with Ms. Holiday.] You know, I think we should quit giving standardized tests. They only reflect a small sampling of what our kids learn and they confuse the parents.

Byers: Don't you think that we as educators should be held accountable?

Green: Of course we should be accountable. But do you honestly feel that a standardized test that was put together by someone who doesn't have the vaguest idea about the kids who go to Dewey should be the measure of how good a job we are doing? Ms. Holiday really threw me off guard when she compared the standardized scores with Mary Ann's report card. Her math test scores were very high, and she only made a C in math. Oh, well, I guess we can just explain it away with the Lake Wobegon effect.

Byers: What does Lake Wobegon have to do with testing?

Green: Have you ever listened to Garrison Keillor's radio show "A Prairie Home Companion"? He talks about the fictitious town of Lake Wobegon. He always says in Lake Wobegon all the men are good looking, all the women are strong, and all the children are above average. I think standardized testing suffers from the Lake Wobegon effect because the expectation is that all students should score above average.

Byers: I really don't think the Lake Wobegon effect applies to Dewey Middle School. But Mary Ann may be a very good test taker. Our new math curriculum and evaluation procedure certainly doesn't give students an opportunity to demonstrate their test-taking skills.

Green: What are you saying?

Byers: I don't know what I'm saying. The fact is that we are mandated to give the standardized tests and report the results. Maybe this would be a good topic for discussion at our next faculty meeting.

Over the next few days, Jane Byers thought about the evaluation procedures that were used at Dewey. Starting in the spring, a series of tests are given—the writing portion of the state test, the state test in reading and math. Eighth graders have to take additional state tests in science and social studies. Students who have taken Algebra I must take a state-required end-of-the-course examination. If that's not enough, a nationally normed standardized achievement test must be given to all students. Jane Byers then remembered the students with individual education programs (IEPs)— they were individually assessed each year. Many of these students took part in the group standardized tests also.

In addition to the state-mandated assessments, each teaching team had devised performance tasks and exhibits to allow students the opportunity to demonstrate what they had learned. For example, in one of the seventh-grade teams, students had to apply what they had learned in math, social studies, and science by collaboratively creating a model of a city at the turn of the century. Many teachers commented that projects such as this reflected what students were actually learning in the classroom rather than the assessment procedure dictating the instruction. There are still some teachers who worry that their students may not be learning what will be on the state tests, however. As a compromise, teachers routinely test students to make sure they are learning the "basics." The grades from the performance tasks and exhibits are averaged with the test grades to get a overall "performance" grade. The performance grade is then averaged with daily work grades to get the report card grade.

Portfolios are sent home to demonstrate to parents the kind of progress their child has made during each 6-week period. Teachers and students together select work to put into the portfolio. For each piece selected, there is a memo attached. The memo includes the date and a brief description of the skill or learning that is demonstrated by the selected piece. The special education consultants help students with IEPs arrange their portfolios to reflect progress toward their short-term objectives and annual goals. The teachers at Dewey made the decision that the portfolio would be the vehicle in which real progress would be documented, but no letter grade or points were given on the portfolio itself. Jane Byers decided to use her time at the next faculty meeting to discuss evaluation procedures. To prepare for the meeting, she researched and listed all evaluation procedures that were currently being used at Dewey. There were more than she realized. She gave each teacher a copy of the list. On a chart, she wrote three questions to stimulate discussion:

1. Why do we evaluate?
2. Who needs to have this information?
3. Are we accomplishing our goal?

She divided the faculty into five groups to brainstorm answers. The brainstorming session provided some interesting revelations: (a) the faculty needed to work more closely together to set standards and criteria for grading work products, and (b) report cards were still based around subjects—a single grade for each subject. Several problems were identified with this method of grading. First, the report card did not reflect the goals the faculty had established for Dewey Middle School:

1. The students at Dewey Middle School will progress toward becoming
   • critical thinkers
   • responsible citizens who give service to their community
   • healthy and fit
   • self-directed learners
2. Each individual student at Dewey Middle School will improve his or her skills in
   • oral literacy
   • written literacy
   • science literacy
   • math literacy
3. Students at Dewey Middle School will have a well-rounded education, which includes knowledge of the arts.
4. Students at Dewey Middle School will demonstrate ethical behavior in all circumstances.

Single grades were also criticized because less-skilled students were being compared with the talented students. In the end, they each received A, B, C, and so forth based on an arbitrary percentage scale. Bill Morris pointed out, "Bob Long can put out almost no effort and still manage to get an A average, whereas Jan Little struggles and works hard, but all she can manage to get is a C."

Tim Jones commented, "If I had only averaged Jan's grades from the last 2 weeks in science, she would have gotten an A. She was finally catching on. Her early grades weren't too good, but she made fantastic progress. I really didn't feel good about giving her a C."

By the end of the meeting, Jane Byers felt a lot had been accomplished. Two committees had been formed to discuss criteria for work products and developing a new report card. Leslie Green spoke up again at the end, "But what about standardized tests? What are we going to do about them?" The others looked around and shrugged their shoulders. It was time to go home.

Questions for Discussion and Activities

1. Discuss and debate the following questions:
   a. What is the purpose of standardized testing? What are the advantages and disadvantages?
   b. Should scores from standardized tests be reported to the general public? Why or why not?
   c. Should test scores be publicized through the news media?
   d. If scores are reported to the general public, do you think there are misperceptions about the reported scores?
   e. Does standardized testing weaken or strengthen curriculum?
   f. Should parents be allowed to refuse permission for their child to participate in standardized testing?
   g. What are the critical points that distinguish scores from grades?
2. Survey a group of teachers and administrators. Ask the following questions:
   a. What is the purpose of evaluating students?
   b. What type of evaluation best suits this purpose?
3. Compare report cards from various school districts. Brainstorm with colleagues ideas for improved methods of reporting progress to different stakeholders (e.g., parents, school administration, news media, legislators).
4. Research the reporting system of your school district. Does it match the school's instructional program and assessment plan?

5. Make recommendations for evaluation procedures at Dewey Middle School.

Relationship to Turning Points Recommendations

- Teach a core academic program
- Ensure success for all students
- Empower teachers and administrators

Recommended Reading

Forte, I., & Schurr, S. (1995). *Making portfolios, products, and performances meaningful and manageable for students and teachers.* Nashville, TN: Incentive.

Herman, J. L., Aschbacher, P. R., & Winters, L. (1992). *A practical guide to alternative assessment.* Alexandria, VA: Association for Supervision and Curriculum Development.

Johnston, P. H. (1992). *Constructive evaluation of literate activity.* White Plains, NY: Longman.

Reporting what students are learning. (1995). *Educational Leadership, 52*(2), 4-58.

Story 16:

But We're Not All Alike

Lea Kowalski turned to face her eighth-grade class. "I'm so excited today! We've all been preparing our immigration or family stories to share with the class. As I look around the room, I see it has turned into a museum. It is wonderful that each of you has taken the time to talk with your family and brought a piece of your family heritage to share with us in class. Each of us needs to learn about the others. We need to be proud of who we are, yet understand each other. I would like you to look for similarities and differences in our stories. As we do so, we will find common threads that bind us all together in this class."

Ben has volunteered to tell his family story first. "I'm going to tell you a story about my grandparents. The year is 1955 and they were both living on farms in Michigan. As they told the story, they were typical teenagers who fell in love, but their parents refused to allow them to marry. They were told they were too young, they had not thought through the community reactions, they were impulsive. Well," Ben continued, "my grandfather is a very stubborn man. He said he would marry grandma no matter what anyone said, and she finally said yes. Here's the kicker. They were married by a justice of the peace in Michigan but drove to Omaha, Nebraska, in separate cars."

"I don't understand," Sue said. "Why would you get married and then drive in separate cars halfway to the west?" "My grandfather is African American," Ben replied, "and my grandmother is of French descent."

"So? I still don't get it," Sue said.

"In 1955, it was a big deal," Ben told her. "They knew that to have an easier life, they needed to move to California. California was more accepting of mixed marriages than Michigan. Although they still faced a lot of prejudice in California. Life has not always been easy for them, but I admire them. I feel they have more courage than most people."

"And I think that was a wonderful story Ben," added Lea Kowalski. "I would say you have good reason to be proud of your grandparents. They were on the cutting edge of changing race relations. Yes, Meagan."

"I'd like to go next. My story is about immigration to the United States." With her teacher's permission, Meagan proceeded. "The year was 1886. My great-great-grandfather chose to emigrate from Germany to the

United States. He was the second of five sons. In Germany, at that time, only the first son would inherent the family estate."

"Why was that?" asked Todd.

"It was the custom," Meagan answered. "The other family members could leave the farm and go to the city, join the military, or work for the eldest son. Well, my grandfather did not like his options. His father decided to offer him another option. The family was fairly well to do and each of the four younger sons were offered $1,000 and passage to the United States. My grandfather took that option. He boarded the ship and sailed to America. He was fortunate. He didn't have to travel in third class, although, he didn't sail first class either. But back to my story. When he made it to Ellis Island, he quickly made it through the inspections. The spelling of his name changed though. The inspectors added an 'e' in the middle."

Confused, Sue asked, "That sounds silly to me. Why would they add a letter to his last name?"

"It was very common to change the spelling of individuals' last names. Remember when we saw the film on Ellis Island?" Lea Kowalski asked. "It referred to how many names were difficult for the inspectors to spell. They would register the person's name the way they heard it. Please continue, Meagan."

"Once he made it off Ellis Island, he boarded a train to Iowa," Meagan said. "Many of his German neighbors had family that settled in southwest Iowa, so he decided to buy land out there. When he made it to the small German community, he felt like he was at home again. It felt good to hear the German language again, speak German again, and eat his ethnic food. Soon after he arrived, he bought land and began to farm in his family's tradition. He was very lonely though. A family that lived a few miles away heard about my great-great-grandfather and decided to set him up with a young German woman living with them. They met at a church social. Well, the rest is history. They were married and had a huge family." Meagan's bright smile demonstrated the pride she had in her family's heritage.

"Thank you, Meagan, for sharing the story of your great-great-grand-father," Lea Kowalski said. "Your story is probably similar to that of many European immigrants. Now, do we have another volunteer today?"

Kim came forward. "I'd like to share my mother's immigration story."

"Good," replied Lea Kowalski. "I'd love to hear her story. Your mother has volunteered so much of her time here at school. She gives wonderful presentations on the many different Asian cultures."

"My mother came to the United States when she was 15 years old," Kim said. "She really didn't choose to come here, but because of family circumstances she had to come. By the time she was 15, both her parents had passed away. She had two younger siblings and nowhere to go in Korea. Her mother's sister lived in Missouri. Aunt Su Lin asked her if she wanted to bring her two younger brothers and come to live with Aunt Su Lin and her husband. My mother's options were few. Her family had always planned for her to get an excellent education, but now she would have to go to work to support her brothers. She decided the best option was to move to the United States. My Great-aunt Su Lin then paid for their flight to St Louis, Missouri. My mother was very scared. She was moving to a new land, leaving the only home she knew, and her English was not fluent. Her brothers, on the other hand, were so excited. They were younger and were going to be adopted by their aunt and uncle.

"Once my mother reached the United States, her aunt went out of her way to make her like the United States. Aunt Su Lin took her everywhere, taught her English so she would not have to be retained in school, and made sure all the neighborhood girls her age would stop by and ask her to do stuff with them. She soon fell in love with her new home. Life has not always been easy for her, but my mom has taught me to be strong and face the challenges that come my way."

"What an interesting story!" Lea Kowalski exclaimed. "Your mom has faced many challenges in her life and has taught you a great lesson. Now, let's take some time to look over our family portraits and relics. Tomorrow, we will continue our family heritage stories."

With that, Lea Kowalski focused her eighth graders on their next activity and hoped that they were gaining as much from hearing family stories as she was.

Questions for Discussion and Activities

1. Suggest other ways the teacher could approach the historical perspective of immigration in a multicultural classroom.
2. Role-play additional family stories and the reactions from the middle school students.
3. Should Lea Kowalski address the underlying issues brought up by each of the student's stories (race relations, family structure, bilingual education, homogeneous and heterogeneous communities)? If so, how could these be done effectively? What issues might emerge in a class discussion? If not, develop support for your position.
4. Develop a lesson plan in the social sciences that addresses diversity in our society.

5. Interview several middle school teachers and discuss possible ways to approach teaching multicultural units in the classroom.

Relationship to Turning Points Recommendations

- Teach core academic program
- Ensure success for all students

Recommended Reading

Banks, J., & Banks, C. (Eds.). (1989). *Multicultural education: Issues and perspectives.* Boston: Allyn & Bacon.

Casanova, U. (1987). Ethnic and cultural differences. In V. Richardson-Koehler (Ed.), *Educators' handbook: A research perspective* (pp. 370-393). New York: Longman

Kozol, J. (1991). *Savage inequalities: Children in America's schools.* New York: Crown.

Story 17:

And the North
Wind Doth Blow

It was a typical spring day in Oakdale. At school, the classroom windows and doors were open because it was so humid. Lunch was over and sixth period had just started. The hour seemed to be going well when someone looked outside and announced it had suddenly grown pitch black!

Within 7 minutes of starting class, the sky had gone from a beautiful blue to a dark, mysterious yellow-green. A siren sounded outside. At about the same moment, Jane Byers came on the intercom and instructed everyone to move from the classrooms to the hallway. Quickly and quietly, the students filed out into the hall. Everyone assumed the tornado emergency position. It was actually impressive. After all the years of practice, these kids knew what was expected of them in a real emergency.

As one looked down the hallway, approximately 200 students were kneeling next to lockers and remaining relatively quiet. The winds began to howl and the classroom doors blew open. The doors had to be locked to keep them from blowing open and possibly hurting someone. It was a nerve-racking experience for everyone. When the winds began to die down a little, Jane Byers came back on the intercom and allowed the students to sit up instead of kneel. It was an uncomfortable experience and many of the students wanted to get up and walk around, but they knew it was in their best interest to stay seated for the time being. The students began to talk to each other, but remained visibly anxious about the situation. No one knew any facts about what was really going on outside in the surrounding area.

A number of students began to weep. The stress had gotten to be too much for them. Many were worried about family members and their homes. Some were afraid they might go home to find the house gone and only a cement slab where once their home had stood.

Teachers tried to console the students. They also watched the sky for signs of a tornado. The sky had lost its darkness for the time being. It seemed to be just an eerie yellow-green color now. Then, out of nowhere, the winds started to howl once more. Instinctively, the students began a domino chain of turning and kneeling. As quiet as it was in the hall, one could hear little prayers and words of encouragement being passed among the classmates. Except for one student . . .

It was at this point that a young man decided he didn't need to be told what to do. He refused to listen to his teacher. It was time to show his independence and express his manhood. Mark had always been an obstinate student, but this was quite the scene. He began to argue with his teacher about having to kneel and cover his head. Soon he was shouting obscenities. This display of behavior was disturbing to the other students, who were unsure how they should react. It was evident that Mark was upsetting his teacher. Her mind had been on the safety and well-being of her infant child at a baby-sitter's home. Now, this 14-year-old was pulling a temper tantrum in the middle of an emergency. The teacher became angry and placed her hand upon Mark's shoulder. She applied pressure as if to push him to the ground.

This action led to another tirade of obscenities and threats. First, Mark was going to sue her for touching him and then he threatened her life. Mark screeched, "Don't you dare touch me, bitch. I'll kill you if you touch me again!" Fortunately, only a few students were fully aware of the confrontation. The whipping wind kept most students' thoughts on their own safety.

When the storm finally passed and the all-clear signal was sounded, students were sent to their seventh-period class, where they would have time to process what had just happened. Mark, however, did not join his classmates. He was on his way to see Jane Byers.

Questions for Discussion and Activities

1. As the classroom teacher, how would you deal with Mark? As the building principal, what would your response be to the altercation which took place?
2. Should other classroom teachers help Mark's teacher with the situation or should they stay with their own classes?
3. If one of the students began to cry and wail uncontrollably during such an event, how would you handle the situation? Remember there are approximately 200 other students in the hallway.
4. How can teachers plan for unexpected behavior in crisis?
5. Are natural disaster and fire drills necessary? Why or why not?
6. Visit a school during a scheduled fire or natural disaster drill. Review existing disaster and evacuation plans. Make any recommendations for improvement you believe are warranted to ensure student safety.

Relationship to **Turning Points** *Recommendations*

- Prepare teachers for the middle level
- Connect schools with communities

Recommended Reading

Muth, K., & Alvermann, D. (1992). *Teaching and learning in the middle grades.* Boston: Allyn & Bacon.

Raebeck, B. (1992). *Transforming middle schools: A guide to whole-school change.* Lancaster, PA: Technomic.

Story 18:

Improving Instruction

Jane Byers finally reached her chair in her office and sat down for the first time that day. It felt more like a week since 7 a.m. when she began. The past few months had been more hectic than usual for everyone at Dewey, but especially for her. Not only was the artist-in-residence program in full swing, but teachers were also asking if meetings were going to be scheduled soon so they could begin to articulate plans for next year. Teacher evaluations were due, and it was only February.

Oh, well, Jane knew that planning early had been part of Dewey's success and she wasn't about to delay work on their 5-year plan just because she had teacher evaluations to do. And the artist-in-residence program, though a drain on everyone's time and energy, was a welcome addition to their curriculum. They had all worked hard to develop the grant, which was funded by the arts council, to bring a series of artists to the school to share their expertise with students. The pointillism project was going exceptionally well, and Jane looked forward to the unveiling of the student-made reproduction of *An Afternoon in the Park*. But still, she had to finish teacher evaluations, and she had to do them well.

"Why didn't I start these earlier this year," Jane lamented. "I promised myself after last year's March marathon that I wouldn't put myself in this predicament again." She knew that she didn't have to do the number of evaluations that had become common practice at Dewey. The district only required that she make three formal observations of nontenured teachers and two of tenured teachers, but she didn't feel she could get to know what really went on in a classroom with so little interaction.

Right from the beginning, Jane had worked to make teachers comfortable with her presence in the classroom. Her regular walk-throughs were now taken for granted. In fact, when teachers didn't see her in the room for a few days, they worried that something was amiss. She had initiated the practice of conducting at least six formal observations for all teachers on review cycle, and she would do more if teachers requested additional observations. At first her plan was quite unpopular, but she felt lucky that over the years the staff had come to value their time together to talk about students, curriculum, and instruction. She took pre- and postobservation conferences seriously. She saw them as an opportunity to not only get to know each teacher better but also as a way to have a direct impact on the school's program. Teachers too had come to value their conferences with her, so planning for tomorrow's postobservation conferences with the two teachers she had observed today would be a serious undertaking.

Jane began with reflecting on the lessons she had observed that day. "What two very different experiences these two observations were today. On the one hand, the 60 minutes with Bill Morris and his eighth graders literally flew by. Students were up and involved, actively participating in every step of the lesson. He opened the lesson with a four-corners technique to get students thinking about the issue of sexual harassment. Students seemed to really enjoy physically moving to one of the four corners of the room to show if they "strongly agreed," "agreed," disagreed,"or "strongly disagreed" with the statement, "Sexual harassment is a problem at Dewey." The activity provided a wonderful preassessment for the lesson and got students thinking about sexual harassment in concrete terms right from the beginning of the lesson. I must remember to ask him to share that technique at the next faculty in-service.

"But that was only the beginning. Bill had a different activity planned every 10 minutes throughout the 60-minute lesson. The use of nominal group technique gave students a chance to think and write on their own, share their thoughts with a partner, and then expand to share their ideas in groups of four, and finally with the whole class."

At that point, Jane took out her script tape of the lesson and noted that Bill only had to make one comment during the entire lesson to redirect a student's attention. "John was the only student that he had to take aside and talk to about his behavior. I wonder if this is typical behavior or if John was having a bad day. I know I haven't seen John in the office for a discipline referral. I wonder if it is because he is carefully monitored by the team."

Jane noted further on her script tape that Bill had reserved the final 5 minutes of class for students to enter summary statements in their journal about what they had learned in the day's lesson. He then outlined the next day's activity, when the whole team would watch a movie on the topic of sexual harassment for the first 50 minutes of their core block. "Real evidence of team planning," thought Jane.

And then there was Martha Docweiler. Jane Byers had resisted the reassignment of Martha Docweiler from the high school to Dewey but accepted the task of working with her to improve instruction when it was inevitable that she would be part of the Dewey team this year. "What a different kind of lesson that was!" Jane recalled her amazement that the seventh graders sat quietly in rows for 45 minutes and completed guided and independent practice on decimals. As in Bill's class, only one student had to be reprimanded for off-task behavior during the entire period. All the rest completed their tasks without cause for teacher intervention. But Jane wondered how engaged students really were in their learning that day.

She thought, "I've observed Martha numerous times, and she consistently maintains an orderly environment. Students appear to be on task when I observe, yet she often complains that students do poorly on her unit tests. Her quarter grades certainly reflect a problem with mastery." Jane pulled out the past quarter's summary report to verify her impressions. "Yes. Martha did have what I would consider an unusually high number of Ds and Fs last quarter, and many were students who performed well in other classes. I have to find a way to get her to think more about her instructional decision-making process and to introduce her to more active strategies to involve students. We'll also need to talk over her plan for the decimal unit to determine if she has ongoing assessment or if she waits until the final unit test to see if students really understand the material."

Jane knew she needed to dedicate the next hour to serious preparation for these two conferences. She checked the outer office. Finding it quiet, she closed her office door and began to finalize her plans for the conferences with these two teachers.

Like Jane Byers, someone else in the building sat at his desk after school to reflect on the day's observation. "I can't believe I really went through with that lesson on sexual harassment for my observation with Jane! What was I thinking! With a sensitive topic like that, anything could have happened. And although I love the four-corners activity, it's so open-ended. I wonder what she thought."

Bill Morris had been through the evaluation cycle with Jane Byers enough times to know that she was fair and professional. He knew that their conference would be productive and that she would find several things that were effective in the lesson. He also knew that her expectations were high for all teachers at Dewey and that she wasn't afraid to raise issues and questions if she thought a particular lesson missed the target. He knew too that she would prompt him for his impressions about the effectiveness of the lesson, and so he knew he had better be well prepared for the postobservation conference the next day.

"When my team decided to use sexual harassment as a thematic organizer for a short integrated unit, I was excited," Bill recalled. "We based our decision to do the unit on our observations of our students, and we knew with certainty that they had much to learn about appropriate and inappropriate behavior with the opposite sex. When we surveyed their parents to see if any of them would come to school to share stories about their understanding and experience with sexual harassment and got such a positive response, we knew that we were on the right track."

Bill reviewed the team's unit plan and noted that five parents were coming to a team meeting next week to share their stories about harassment in the workplace with students. He was looking forward to this activity and knew that along with his students he would benefit from time to interact with parents about this topic. He also noted that the social skill the team had decided to integrate into the unit was one the students needed to practice a lot. Not many of the eighth graders had yet mastered how to be assertive without resorting to aggression, and their advisory activities throughout the unit that focused on this social skill were sure to raise some interesting issues. His review of the team's plan assured him that their unit on sexual harassment had been well thought out and researched and he planned to share a copy with Jane in the postobservation conference.

"I feel students were actively involved throughout the lesson," Bill thought, "although John really frustrated me today with his behavior. He seems to be getting more and more agitated. I need to add him to our team meeting agenda for Wednesday so I can find out from others if they have observed the same behavior in their classes. Otherwise, I think my plan to change activities every 10 minutes kept the students busy and involved."

There still lingered some doubt that maybe he had crammed too much into one lesson. "Maybe," he thought, "changing activities too often is worse than not changing at all. Did I create chaos instead of classroom energy? Did students really benefit from all of the activities?"

When Bill was roused from his reverie by a colleague at the door, he promised himself that he would reserve time at home that night to finish his own evaluation of the day's observation so that he would be well prepared for the conference in the morning with Jane.

Upstairs, Martha Docweiler ran into John Graber on her way out to her car and stopped to talk, because she knew if she didn't, John would make sure she paid for her oversight. John didn't like to be ignored, and most people in the building tolerated him, admitting that sometimes they agreed with him, even though his attitude and reputation had pitted him against almost everyone on the staff at one time or another.

"So, you're leaving already, Martha," John asked, knowing full well that her packed bag and coat meant that she was headed out the door.

"Yes. I have a few errands to run tonight before I go home," Martha answered, "and I'm afraid I can't wait until the weekend to get them done." Holding up her bag, she assured him, "I'll just have to finish my work for tomorrow this evening."

"Well, what work do you have to do that's so important?" queried John. "They don't pay me enough to do work at home in the evening."

And at this point, Martha accepted that she probably wouldn't get all of her errands done tonight. "Well, I have my usual set of math papers to grade and I also have to prepare for a postobservation conference with Jane tomorrow morning. She observed my seventh-grade math class today, and you know how she likes us to think about our lesson before we meet with her."

"Well, I'll say. She can be so picky on teacher evaluations! Why does she think we need six observations, when everyone else in the district can get the job done with only two or three? Oh, yes. I've had a problem with her coming into my classroom all along, but nobody seems to want to listen to me."

"Oh no. Here we go again," thought Martha. "John jumps on his bandwagon to criticize Jane every chance he gets, and I'm not in the mood for him today." She recalled her experiences with past principals who would observe her class the minimum amount of time, give an opinion of the lesson, fill out the required paperwork, and be done with it. She didn't really care what her evaluations said. She knew she was an excellent teacher and that her reputation just wasn't fair. But she had to admit Jane had forced her to think more about instruction in the last few years than she ever had before. She still maintained that she knew what she was doing in the classroom and especially how to make seventh graders toe the line.

"You know, John," she said now, "I've taught for 23 years, and I know how to get kids to behave in class. Like today, for example, except for Tim, who is just a nuisance and should be placed in a special education class, not one student was off task the entire lesson. I had them working so hard they barely had time to breathe. Jane won't have any problem with my lesson today. I had those kids under control." And with that, Martha turned and made her way to the car so she could escape John's watchful eye and finally get started on those errands that she just had to get done.

For Jane Byers, Bill Morris, and Martha Docweiler, the next morning would come quickly. Each in his or her own way would spend time that evening to be sure to be prepared for their face-to-face dialogue about effective instruction in the classroom.

Questions for Discussion and Activities

1. Prepare for the postobservation conferences to be held tomorrow morning between Jane Byers and Bill Morris, and Jane Byers and Martha Docweiler.

   a. What are your impressions of the approach Jane Byers takes to staff evaluation? Does research support her practice of frequent observations? Is there any research that supports her conferencing strategy to actively involve teachers in self-evaluation?

   b. What was your impression of Bill Morris's lesson? What is a four-corners activity? How could it be used in a middle school classroom? What other active instructional strategies could Bill Morris have used during the lesson? What was your impression of his summarizing activity?

   c. What was your impression of Martha Docweiler's lesson? How and when can guided and independent practice be used effectively? Was Martha Docweiler's lesson effective because students did not disrupt the class? Do you agree with Jane Byers that more active student involvement is needed in Martha Docweiler's classroom? How would you account for the high number of Ds and Fs in Martha Docweiler's class?

2. Assume the role of Jane Byers. How would you conduct a postobservation conference with each teacher? What issues would you raise for discussion?

3. Role-play the postobservation conferences with each teacher. Rotate roles and discuss your perceptions of Jane Byers, Bill Morris, and Martha Docweiler. How would your perception of teaching effectiveness vary according to the perspective of each individual?

Relationship to Turning Points Recommendations

- Ensure success for all students
- Empower teachers and administrators
- Prepare teachers for the middle grades

Recommended Reading

Breeden, T., & Egan, E. (1995). *Strategies and activities to raise student achievement.* Nashville, TN: Incentive.

George, P., & Alexander, W. (1993). *The exemplary middle school.* New York: Harcourt Brace Jovanovich.

George, P., Stevenson, C., Thomason, J., & Beane, J. (1992). *The middle school and beyond.* Alexandria, VA: Association for Supervision and Curriculum Development.

Irvin, J. (1992). Developmentally appropriate instruction: The heart of the middle school. In J. Irvin (Ed.), *Transforming middle level education: Perspectives and possibilities* (pp. 295-313). Boston: Allyn & Bacon.

Merenbloom, E. (1988). *Developing effective middle schools through faculty participation* (2nd ed.). Columbus, OH: National Middle School Association.

Stronge, J., & Jones, C. (1991). Middle school climate: The principal's role in influencing effectiveness. *Middle School Journal, 22*(5), 41-46.

Vitale, B. (1982). *Unicorns are real.* Rolling Hills Estates, CA: Jalmar.

Wood, K. (1994). *Practical strategies for improving instruction.* Columbus, OH: National Middle School Association.

Story 19:

How Long Does It Have to Be?

> At 7:30 p.m. on Monday, February 21, 1983, twelve professors from the English and Education Departments at the University of New Hampshire met to examine the writing of one middle school teacher's students. They had heard about the writing of these children and wanted to see for themselves. The teacher was Nancie Atwell from the small town of Boothbay Harbor, Maine. I was fortunate enough to be one of those professors who sat in a circle randomly perusing the mass of student folders from a large box on the floor.
>
> I remember looking across the circle at Don Murray, who shook his head as if to say, "Can you believe this?" The variety of student voices, range of genres, uses of writing, and experimentations were of a quality few of us had ever seen before. (p. iii)

Thus begins Donald Graves's foreword to Nancie Atwell's book *In the Middle.* Since its publication in 1987, this book has begun to revolutionize the teaching of writing in middle schools. Commonsense writing strategies are described through the lens of an exceptional teacher as she works with "typical" eighth graders. Many, many teachers have taken this book to heart and re-created their language arts classrooms. But change in language arts instruction, the bedrock of a traditional curriculum, comes slowly. The following story illustrates the conflict between new ideas and tradition.

Richard Hoff heard the distinct *ding, ding* of a front-desk bell as he walked down the hall toward Emily Pritchart's room. "What on earth is she doing now?" he wondered, as he strode into her eighth-grade language arts class. He swept his eyes across the fairly quiet if somewhat chaotic classroom. "Where the devil is she?" Finally he spotted her, seated next to a student's desk on a low stool. Both she and the student were intently looking at a paper, talking quietly. Actually, she appeared to be listening more than talking as the student talked animatedly and pointed several times at the paper—the center of their attention.

"She's oblivious to the rest of the class," thought Richard Hoff as he approached the huddled couple and noticed that the student was Sammy Smith, from the low-track experimental group that Emily Pritchart insisted on having integrated into her regular-track language arts. "She's probably regretting that now, having to spend all of her time with this student to the neglect of the other, better students."

Just as he was about to call her name the bell rang out again. All heads lifted briefly as Suzy Jones spoke to the class. "Could I get some response to this paper? I think I've fixed most of the problems I've been having with it."

"Now Emily Pritchart will have to get to work," thought Richard Hoff. To his amazement, she turned immediately back to Sammy, but several of the students in the class abandoned their work to join Suzy at a table in the corner of the room. "What's going on here?" Richard decided to take a closer look around the room. Emily saw him looking around, but as he didn't seem to want to speak with her she continued to listen to Sammy explain the various problems he was having with a letter he was writing to the local YMCA.

"I want to make them understand how what I'm suggesting can help everyone," Sammy reasoned. "How does this sound?"

If you allow us to hold our eighth-grade paper drive on your parking lot every Saturday during the month of April, we won't be causing trouble in the streets downtown.

"Is the purpose of the paper drive to keep eighth graders off the streets?" asked Emily.

"No, it's to raise money for new soccer balls and nets. You know that, Ms. Pritchart," Sammy responded, looking into her questioning eyes. "Oh, I get it. You know that, but they won't unless I tell them. Yeah, what if I move this part up here?" He circled a large section of his paper and drew an arrow to the very beginning of the page. He read over his paper and grinned. "That's better. Thanks, Ms. Pritchart. Let me work on this a little more, then I'd like to share it with you again before I take it to my response group."

Emily Pritchart rose from the stool and surveyed the room. She smiled with some pride as she watched the eighth-grade writing workshop moving along smoothly. Suzy's response group was in the midst of an animated discussion. She knew that Suzy could hold her own and retain control of her writing even while considering the suggestions of her peers. "I wish all of the peer response groups worked that smoothly," thought Emily. "But give 'em time."

Most of the other students were working independently on a variety of pieces of writing. Emily looked at the large wall chart on which the students had scribbled in their writing plans for the morning. "Let's see, rough draft of a new piece for Tommy. Janell is still reworking that piece for the school newspaper. Bill is revising, for the fifth time, his story about winning the big game. I need to urge him to finish up or move on. He set a goal to write more pieces this grading period. He's not going to reach his goal at this pace. He's signed up for a conference with me at 10. I'll talk to him then. Meanwhile, I wonder how the play group is getting along?"

She crossed the room to look in on the five students who were writing a play to perform for the upcoming Snowball. She was proud of all the research the group had done on drug abuse as they prepared to write this play. They were trying out lines and making revisions based on how they thought their middle school audience would respond. She listened in for a while. Suddenly, Jane, another of her low-track writers, reminded the group that their play would also be performed in several of the grade schools.

"They're our audience, too." Jane said. "We have to consider them. They won't understand that last part. We have to find a way to say the same thing in simpler words." Emily smiled as she listened in, knowing she wasn't really needed there either.

"Ms. Pritchart,"interrupted Richard Hoff. "Ms. Pritchart, exactly what was your lesson plan for this morning's language arts block? Your students seem to be scattered all over doing a variety of things, including sharing their work with each other! Meanwhile, you seem to be spending an inordinate amount of time with one student or wandering around the room casting an approving eye on all this jumble."

"Listen Mr. Hoff," Emily replied. "Welcome to eighth-grade writing workshop. This is how it's supposed to look. The students are writing about things that interest them. They're writing things that need to be written for audiences that are interested in what they have to say."

"Yes, but what about our prepared curriculum?" Richard asked. "What about grammar and spelling? And I've seen some terrible penmanship as I've walked around this room. How do you ever read it?"

"I probably won't read it in that form," Emily told him. "The students' rough drafts are just that—rough. They'll be cleaned up before I ever see them. You see, the students help each other with their writing. That's what Suzy's response group is doing. And over there, Phil and James are editing each other's papers for history class."

"But this is language arts class," Richard objected. "Shouldn't they be working on a piece for you? And how can these low-track students help anyone? They can barely help themselves."

"Listen, all of these students have something to say. My writing workshop gives them an opportunity to say it. We're a community. We help each other, and we're growing together. Not all at the same rate, not all with the same level of success, but we're all moving ahead."

"Well, we'll see about that when the test scores come back! We'll see then about this newfangled workshop. Looks like a free-for-all to me." Richard strode from the classroom casting one more disgusted look in Emily's direction. She sighed—and then, *ding, ding, ding,* the response group bell rang out.

Questions for Discussion and Activities

1. Why was Richard Hoff so frustrated when he couldn't spot Emily Pritchart the moment he entered her classroom?
2. Is it fair for Emily Pritchart to spend so much individual time with her "low-track" students? Explain your view of equity in the classroom.
3. Why do you think that Emily Pritchart had so many different writing assignments going on at the same time?
4. From this story, what are some of the characteristics of the writing workshop?
5. How and why would this teaching strategy fit the characteristics of middle grade students?
6. Why do you think Richard Hoff is skeptical of this "newfangled" approach?
7. How can language arts content be taught through the writing workshop approach? How do you think students will do on the tests that Richard Hoff alluded to?
8. Brainstorm a list of the kinds of lessons you remember doing in eighth-grade language arts. How does your list differ from Emily Pritchart's writing workshop?
9. Brainstorm ways that students can help one another with writing in an untracked classroom.
10. If you were going to establish a writing workshop, how would you set up your classroom? Draw a floor plan.
11. What kind of organizational aids would a workshop teacher need to devise to keep track of students? What do you think Emily Pritchart's chart looked like? Draw a picture.

Relationship to **Turning Points** *Recommendations*

- Create small communities for learning
- Teach a core academic program
- Ensure success for all students
- Empower teachers and administrators
- Connect schools with communities

Reference and Recommended Reading

Atwell, N. (1987). *In the middle: Writing, reading, and learning with adolescents.* Portsmouth, NH: Heinemann.

Facing Challenges From the Outside

5

Story 20:

When Trouble Hits

In the media center at Dewey, faculty are seated around the tables normally occupied at this early hour by students with permission to work on projects before school begins. These tables are situated between the reference collection and the checkout desk, where the media center director can watch student activities. The media center is large, its ceilings high, its plain cream-colored walls decorated with posters proclaiming the virtues of learning. Large windows at the south end open on the landscaped lawn, allowing natural light to illuminate the room. This pleasant room is normally alive with energy throughout the day as students prepare for presentations and class projects.

Most of the people in the chairs around the tables this morning are faculty. Ken Wilson noted, however, that not all the teachers had arrived yet even though it was close to the time for the first bell. Sounds of serious conversation drifted to Ken from the tables near him. Some, like Harriet Plumber, apparently knew what had happened and were enjoying the attention of colleagues engrossed in every word she spoke. Ken wished he had listened to the radio on the way to school this morning instead of going through his usual routine of running through his plans for the day in his head to make sure he hadn't forgotten anything. He was nervous after being greeted at the locked door by a police officer with a dog who refused to let him in without checking his school identification, which he always carried in his wallet.

"Is there a problem?" Ken had inquired while fumbling through his wallet trying to locate the ID.

"All teachers are to report to the media center immediately," the officer had responded, glancing at Ken's face after examining the photo on the ID.

Ken noticed on his way to the media center that small groups of students sat in the cafeteria, not nearly as many as there should be this close to the beginning bell. In the media center, Ken hunched forward in his chair like somebody communicating that he's trying to watch TV around a distraction, trying to listen in to the group of people adjacent to him, who were so engrossed in their conversation they did not see Richard Hoff, the assistant principal, walk in. Conversations continued as Richard greeted teachers and glanced around for a place to position himself.

"The Ku Klux Klan is gathering at the lake tonight," someone said at the next table.

"I hear the Black Panthers were supposed to be meeting at the lake," someone else added.

"But what does that have to do with us?" Ken thought to himself as he listened.

"Who said the first white teacher who arrived at school today would be shot?" another person asked.

"Well, why else would the police be here?" someone answered.

"I didn't hear that, but I did hear that the first white student leaving the school today would be shot," said May Spencer, the media center supervisor. She went on to proclaim that a gang of whites had promised to beat up black students as they walked home if anything happened to any whites. Ken was baffled.

"As most of you know, we have a serious problem on our hands right now," he heard Richard Hoff announce. "Last Friday evening, Mike Madison, a student who had recently transferred here from Tyler Middle School, was shot and killed in what appears to have been an accident but is being played out as a racial incident because three white students are being charged with involuntary manslaughter."

Ken was startled. Mike Madison had only been at Dewey for 8 days. He came from one of the other district middle schools, where his involvement with a group of older boys was reputed to be the cause of three suspensions. He had a reputation for insolence, apathy, and everything else that irritates teachers and culminated in absolute failure in all subjects. His father, a black minister at the African New Covenant Church, had pressured the superintendent to allow Mike to be admitted to Dewey in an attempt to remove him from an undesirable element and renew his interest in academics.

Persuaded to accept him on their team, Ken had found Mike to be a very personable and likable student. Originally, he had opposed placing Mike on any team because of the reputation that preceded him from Tyler Middle School. "We've spent 6 months nurturing an open, safe and cooperative learning environment," he had argued. "I don't think we should sacrifice this for anyone, especially for someone students will be afraid of and who is likely to drain the energies of the whole team."

Richard Hoff continued to discuss the details surrounding the shooting of the student and why they needed to brace for potential racial incidents among the students in school as well as from those outside the school who had threatened to retaliate. "We expect at all three middle schools only 40% to 50% of the students will attend school today, and we do not expect attendance to normalize until the tension recedes. As you can tell, we also have a lot of teachers who stayed home this morning. Because of the nature of the crisis, our attempt at getting substitutes has been unsuccessful. Instead of bringing in substitutes, we are asking you to make adjustments to accommodate the students who are present today. I understand there were not many who arrived on the first set of buses."

"Why don't we just shut the school down until this all cools off?" Ken asked.

"Because the superintendent doesn't believe we should make more out of this than it actually was. We believe it was an accident and not racially motivated and that we should act accordingly," the assistant principal replied.

"Richard?" Barbara Peck asked. "I heard that black gangs from around the state have been asked to come and help riot and ransack this school. Is this true?"

"What about the phone call Jane got Sunday morning?" interrupted Bob Knoble, who always knew more than anyone else when something happened in the district. "I understand that the caller was a black man who announced they were going to shoot the first white teacher who stepped out of this school building." After pausing until he sensed the full effect of what he said had registered with everyone, he went on. "Didn't you notice the cars cruising the streets in front of the school when you came in? I think it's foolish to keep this school open and risk the teachers' lives. They could just drive by and shoot through the windows and kill any one of us."

From his astonished expression, it was hard to believe the assistant principal had heard these rumors. Bob suggested to the group that perhaps Richard Hoff had been asked to call this meeting to divert teachers' attention from a meeting of the principal and other district administrators with the police, the mayor, city council members, and black community leaders. "They have been meeting all weekend trying to make sense out of the shooting death of the 15-year-old," reported Bob.

"I cannot confirm or deny any of these rumors," was all Richard said. He went on to say, "I can tell you that the school district is making arrangements for 5 to 10 additional counselors and psychologists to meet with small groups of students today. They will be available here all week to meet with any student who asks to talk to them. Please be sensitive and allow students access to them when they ask."

"I am supposed to supervise the intramural softball game on the playground during the activity period today," Ken mentioned. "Do you think I should keep everyone in?"

The assistant principal took off his glasses and rubbed his eyes. He looked frustrated. "Mr. Wilson," he said, "Do I have to tell you everything to do? Don't you think you and your team members are capable of making that decision?" With that, Richard Hoff closed off further discussion by the teachers and announced that they were to have team meetings at the beginning and end of each day to enable them to plan appropriately for the week. The team leaders were requested to contact all absent teachers and encourage them to return.

At the end of the day, Ken and the other two members of the Yellow Fellows team who had come to school met to plan the week. Considering what could have happened, he felt the day had gone pretty well. No drive-by shootings had occurred. The students had insisted on going outside for the softball activity. Accompanied by a police officer and his German Shepherd dog, they marched out to the softball field. Ken had remained close to the officer, glancing up and down the street, suspicious of every car that passed and wondering how he would react if he saw a gun pointing from the window. He never did organize the teams, and the students, who had insisted in going out to play the game, were too interested in petting the dog and talking to police officers to care.

Gayle Huin was the only Yellow Fellow team member who did not show that day. She agreed to come in on Tuesday, provided there were no incidents and the police were still in the building. Ken convinced her to return by telling her how cooperative and considerate both the students and teachers had been throughout the day. He said it was actually exciting. He never would have thought they could be so creative with teaching during a crisis. He admitted that some former students had been able to talk their way into the locked school but were quickly spotted and removed by the police. "I hate to say it," he told her, "but this incident has gotten this team and other teams really pulling together."

Not having time to prepare an agenda, Ken opened the meeting informally. "Basically," he began, "we have to decide what and how to teach with police and dogs patrolling the halls, a team of counselors and psychologists set up to talk with any student who asks, rumors of shooting, and the potential for violence to erupt among students at any time."

"The first thing I think we should decide," Mary Allen said, "is how are we going to handle student requests to see a counselor. Do we have to let them go any time they ask?"

"Okay, that's a good point, Mary," Ken said. "We'll discuss that. What else?"

"As we don't know how many students are going to be in school, how are we supposed to handle makeup work?" Bill Walker asked.

"I think we should continue to set aside our usual plans and develop content around what has been happening and what the students are presently experiencing," Ken responded.

Questions for Discussion and Activities

1. What is the role of counselors during a time of crisis?
2. Brainstorm a list of interdisciplinary activities and ideas for teaching content related to a crisis such as this.
3. Role-play a group discussion between key community leaders.
   a. Identify community leaders who would be needed at a deliberation about this incident.
   b. Include in your scenario possible issues of concern for each constituency group and how those concerns might be addressed in the school and community.

Relationship to Turning Points *Recommendations*

- Empower teachers and administrators
- Connect schools with communities

Recommended Reading

Jacobs, H. (Ed.). (1989). *Interdisciplinary curriculum: Design and implementation.* Alexandria, VA: Association for Supervision and Curriculum Development.

National Middle School Association. (1991). *Treasure chest: A teacher advisory resource book.* Macon, GA: Panaprint.

Shur, S. (1989). *Dynamite in the classroom: A how-to handbook for teachers.* Columbus, OH: National Middle School Association.

Story 21:

Parent-Teacher Conferences: The Good, the Bad, and the Ugly

12:30 p.m. Emily Pritchart sits alone at her desk using her lunch hour to prepare for the parent-teacher conferences scheduled later in the afternoon. As team leader, she knows that she will be primarily responsible to conduct the conferences, though her teammates will be present and will offer input when needed. Smiling, she chastises herself for feeling butterflies in her stomach just thinking about these conferences. After all, she's been doing them for over 10 years. But maybe her experience actually contributes to her nervousness. Over the years, she has been disappointed, encouraged, angered, delighted, and depressed by her contacts with parents. She has also been surprised. Often, when she based her expectations about parents on her impressions of their eighth-grade children, she had been dead wrong.

Emily knows how important families are to the well-being of the students on her team. And even though her students often act as if they want a divorce from their parents, she knows that they still need strong parental support. She knows too that she—and the school—need the support of parents as well.

What will today's conferences be like? There are two that she's particularly worried about.

First, there's Johnny Smith. How should she approach the Smiths about Johnny? Johnny works hard, but he seems to be at such loose ends all the time. He's disorganized, late with most assignments, and easily distracted and therefore falling behind in most of his course work. Her teammates think he's scatterbrained and shallow, but Emily wants to look deeper.

Then, there's Claire Connor. What was it that troubled Emily about Claire? She's quiet. She's always trying to please. As a matter of fact, she tries too hard to please everyone all of the time. She's kind of nervous, too. She closes herself off from teachers and other students. She doesn't have any friends. There's something sad about her. Do her parents see these same traits at home? Do they share Emily's concerns?

3:10 p.m. Mr. and Ms. Smith enter the team room like they were shot out of a circus cannon—all energy and very little impact. Mr. Smith immediately looks at his watch. "I'm sorry we're late, but I simply had to finish up some things at work before we could come. And unfortunately, we'll have to make this quick as I have a 3:30 tee time and the missus has to take Johnny to swim team practice. We've got high hopes for Johnny's future as an Olympic swimmer. Those daily 6 a.m. workouts have taken seconds off his lap times."

Ms. Smith speaks up in a determined tone, "We're not at all happy with the reports we're getting about Johnny's falling grades. Not acceptable, simply not acceptable."

"What my wife is trying to say," interrupts Mr. Smith, "is that Johnny will never get into a Big 10 school with the grades he's been getting lately. It's never too early to begin thinking about college, you know."

Her teammates nervously look to Emily to respond, and finally she sees an opening. "Yes, Mr. Smith, my teammates and I are also concerned about Johnny's slipping grades. And I must say we're a bit puzzled. Johnny appears to be working all the time, but he seldom completes any tasks. And when he does complete them, they're poorly done. For the most part, the work he is able to complete in class is fine, but when he has to take work home the results are almost always disappointing."

"He never mentions having homework while we're on the way to swim team practice. Does he have homework every night?" asks Ms. Smith.

"Not every night, but several times a week," answers Emily. "Homework helps students learn responsibility. It also provides an opportunity for parents to take an active interest in their child's education."

"Take an interest!" erupts Mr. Smith. "My wife and I devote plenty of time to our son. I work 60 hours a week taking an interest in putting bread on the table, dressing my son like a fashion model, and paying for swim team and piano lessons and tennis lessons. And my wife is little more than a taxi service driving Johnny all over creation. I think this school simply expects too much out of 14-year-olds."

Mr. Smith rages on for several more minutes, talking about all the sacrifices he and his wife have made so Johnny can make something of himself. He talks more about the plans they've made for Johnny. He describes how every minute of every day of Johnny's life is filled with activities that will prepare him for a brilliant future.

Finally, Emily interrupts again. "What will happen to all of these plans if Johnny keeps falling further behind in school? Johnny needs your help with his schoolwork."

"That's my wife's department," responds Mr. Smith. "Besides, I'll be late for golf."

"What can I do to help?" Ms. Smith asks as her husband leaves the team room.

The team begins to tell her about their plan to monitor homework by . . .

3:35 p.m. Claire's father walks slowly into the team room, shoulders slumped, head down. He reminds Emily of Claire—that's how she enters the classroom every day.

"Claire's a good girl," Mr. Connor begins. "She helps out a lot at home. Cooks supper most nights and then cleans up. You see, her mom don't feel well most of the time. I don't know what I'd do without Claire to take care of things. She's real good with her younger brothers and sisters, too."

"You're right," says Emily, "Claire is a good girl. She tries very hard to please her teachers here at school. But I'm worried about Claire. She doesn't seem very happy. She seems like she's troubled about something. I was hoping you could help me understand why Claire is so difficult to get to know."

Jack Caulder adds that he has noticed Claire's demeanor and attitude in his classes as well and he wants to know how he could help her open up more in class.

"What has Claire told you?" Mr. Connor asks.

"That's just it. She hasn't said anything, Mr. Connor," responds Emily. "I was hoping you would tell me how I—we—can help Claire."

Mr. Connor's voice breaks as he begins to tell a painful story about his wife's addiction to alcohol; how Claire and he try to keep things afloat at home; and how mean, even cruel, his wife can be when she's been drinking. "I had no idea that all of this was troubling Claire. She never complains about anything, just always tries to help out," sighs Claire's father. "What can I do? I don't want Claire burdened with all of this."

Emily and Jack begin to tell Mr. Connor about . . .

4:30 p.m. The team sits together in the team room, drained and exhausted, but somehow energized by these contacts with parents.

Questions for Discussion and Activities

1. Describe some of the school or community programs Emily Pritchart might have offered Ms. Smith and Mr. Connor.
2. Other than established programs, what can the team recommend to these parents? How can they help parents help their children through their preadolescence?

3. Ask a middle school teacher how she or he might respond to these two situations. What programs does your placement middle school provide for students who are failing? What programs are available in your community to support Claire and her father?

4. Role-play additional parent-teacher conferences. Pick another student described in one of the other cases. How might a conference with his or her parents sound?

5. This case doesn't describe an entire parent-teacher conference. What components should be a part of every conference? Should the student be included in all conferences? How should teachers begin?

Relationship to Turning Points *Recommendations*

- Engage families
- Connect schools with communities

Recommended Reading

Beane, J., & Lipka, R. (1987). *When the kids come first: Enhancing self-esteem.* Columbus, OH: National Middle School Association.

Elkind, D. (1969). *The hurried child. Reading*, MA: Addison-Wesley.

Glasser, W. (1969). *Schools without failure.* New York: Happer& Row.

Johnstone, J. H. (1990). *The new American family and the school.* Columbus, OH: National Middle School Association.

Story 22:

More Than Dollars

Sonia watched Carl for a few moments as their bus proceeded slowly down the road. Even stopping to pick up more students did not seem to shake Carl from his reverie. Finally she asked, "Why so silent today?"

Carl glanced behind him at Sonia and replied, "Just thinking about my days at Dewey. A lot has happened since I've been here."

Noticing that he was a bit more dressed up than usual, Sonia commented, "Are you a tour guide today, too?"

As Carl nodded, she added, "I can't wait to get out of class to show next year's sixth graders around today when they visit our school. It's great to be chosen, don't you think?"

Carl did feel honored, but most of all he was amazed that he was asked to lead a group of students through "his" school and share his impressions. To Sonia he said, "Yeah, I'm glad they asked me, but I really don't get it. I only came here in the middle of last year and I got off to kind of a bad start."

"What do you mean?" questioned Sonia. "We were on different teams last year and I didn't see you much. Was it hard for you to pick up in the middle of the year?"

Not only had it been difficult for Carl to change schools midyear, but many other things had changed for Carl, too. Just before Christmas, his parents had decided to get a divorce. Carl, his mom, and his younger sister had moved from the only home he had ever known to this town where his mother had been raised. He knew she wanted to be nearer to her parents and that she could find work more easily here than in the small town where they had lived, but he had not wanted to move. The adjustment had been much harder for Carl than for his third-grade sister. In fact, she seemed to fit right in and actually liked her new school. Not so for Carl. Accepting his new environment took a long time and required a lot of effort on the part of others, too.

But how could Sonia understand? She was perky, popular, and always seemed to be the center of attention. She probably wouldn't want to hear about his early struggles, and he really didn't have time to say much, as the bus would be arriving at school soon. When he hesitated, Sonia added, "I remember being so happy for you last year because you got a PALS partner. My neighbor, Mr. Thompson, was your mentor and you two seemed to have such fun together. Isn't he special?"

Carl wondered how she knew about the Partners Acting as Links for Students (PALS) program, but he replied, "Mr. Thompson is one of the best friends a guy could have. I gave him a hard time at first, but he didn't give up on me. He took me fishing, bowling, to the water park, and he even helped me build a dog house for my new dog. So how do you know about the PALS program?"

Sonia proceeded to explain that as a sixth grader, she was asked to be one of three student representatives on a committee that was formed to explore how to link community resources with school-related needs. The adult members originally focused on ways to form business partnerships with companies to gain financial support, and how to involve parent and community volunteers. Sonia somewhat smugly acknowledged that she and the other students had kept some goals centered on individual students' needs.

One program that resulted was PALS. Community members, such as the local hardware-store owner Mr. Thompson, had been recruited and trained to be mentors for students with special social or emotional needs. Carl qualified because he was a midyear transfer student and his counselor felt he could use the extra attention. Sonia's aunt, who lived on the West Coast, had helped form a similar group in her community and had willingly shared ideas and materials.

Sonia could have talked all day about her involvement on the community resources committee, but the bus had stopped in the school drive and the students were departing. Carl hopped off the bus after Sonia and smiled good-bye. They both prepared to greet the visitors who would be eager to hear about life at Dewey from another student's perspective.

Questions for Discussion and Activities

1. Other than financial support, for what reasons might a business or industry be contacted by school personnel?
2. Identify some goals for a program like PALS.
   a. What kind of selection process would be needed for students and adult volunteers?
   b. What training and guidelines would be essential?
   c. How can the time for termination of the student-mentor relationship be determined?

d. What are the advantages and disadvantages of this type of program?

3. Contact at least three schools to gather information on their parent and community volunteer programs.
   a. List the tasks performed by the volunteers.
   b. Is there a written handbook for the volunteers?
   c. What recognition is given to volunteers?

4. Identify other community resources and agencies that work with schools.

5. What is your impression of using students as part of an orientation program for incoming sixth graders? What could students do other than lead tours to help new students acclimate to the school? What other issues need to be considered to help make the transition from fifth to sixth grade a smooth one?

Relationship to Turning Points Recommendations

- Reengage families in the education of young adolescents
- Connect schools with communities

Recommended Reading

Bernick, R., & Rutherford, B. (1993). *Connecting school family community resources* (School and Family Partnership Series). Denver: RMC Research.

Cooley, V. E. (1993). Tips for implementing a student assistance program. *NASSP Bulletin, 76*(549), 10-20.

Dykeman, C. (1994, July). *Student assistance program implementation and evaluation.* Paper presented at the International Conference on Counseling in the 21st Century, Vancouver, British Columbia.

Johnstone, J. H. (1990). *The new American family and the school.* Columbus, OH: National Middle School Association.

Kotloff, L. J. (1993). *Comparative case studies of five peer support group programs.* Philadelphia: Public/Private Ventures.

Waggoner, J. E. (1995, February). *Adolescents in crisis: Implementing Carnegie recommendations in middle level teacher education by collaborating with community service agencies.* Paper presented at the 75th annual meeting of the Association of Teacher Educators, Detroit.

Wiehe, J. A. (1993). *Piecing together an integrated approach to drug-free schools.* Austin: Austin Independent School District, Texas Office of Research and Evaluation.

Story 23:

Networking for Support

Judy McKay scans the faces of the visitors seated around the tables in the media center. As she tries to read their body language, her thoughts drift to 4 years earlier when she was on the teacher team that visited Hamilton Middle School, Dewey's mentor school. That was the landmark day when she began to understand and accept middle school concepts.

Faculties at Dewey and Hamilton are fortunate to be located in a state where the middle school association sponsors a partnership service to member schools, pairing model and demonstration middle schools with other schools at the beginning stages of involvement. Demonstration schools send speakers to help with in-service sessions and also encourage site visits for staff to experience a middle school in action. And of course, when questions arise, they are only a phone call or fax message away.

Membership benefits in the middle school association also include ongoing support from the director and staff members. They remain on call to answer questions, attend meetings as speakers or consultants, and serve as a referral service to connect schools with similar concerns or problems. Fall, spring, and summer statewide conferences provide teachers and administrators with valuable workshop information and the opportunity to network and share ideas with middle school comrades.

Now, after only 4 years, Dewey has achieved the distinction of being a demonstration school, partnered with Pine Lake Middle School, just 185 miles away. About half of Pine Lake's staff were able to spend the day at Dewey and the summary session is about to begin.

As the chair of the coordinating council, Judy McKay addresses the assembled group. The school pride she feels is evident to all. But clearly, she is also a realist who knows that good middle schools keep changing and improving. Judy and the four other Dewey staff members who are present encourage their visitors to ask questions, make comments, and share observations. She acknowledges that this is an open, sharing environment. Dewey personnel intend to grow from the feedback. After all, in a partnership, both schools can benefit.

Early in the discussion, the comments center around the positive learning styles observed, the many reward systems in use, the friendliness of students and staff, the noise level in the halls, and some of the interdisciplinary units being taught or planned. Then, the visitors share the results of the survey questions that they compiled. Included were questions such as:

- What do you like/dislike most about this school?
- Who makes decisions at this school?
- How can you tell if students are learning?
- What effective classroom management techniques are used by your team?
- How do you feel about being part of a team?

While answers to these and other questions are shared, Judy retrieved her staff development notebook and made careful notes. Her reputation for being well organized is legendary at Dewey. After her first middle school visit, Judy was determined to maintain thorough files for her growing collection of middle school materials. Her single subdivided notebook soon gave way to individually titled ones for teaming, advisory, adolescent development, integrated curriculum, and community resources. Today's notes just might become the basis for some in-service training.

As Judy wrote and reflected on the day's insights, she was once again overwhelmed by feelings of connectedness to other educators who seem to truly care about the kids. Searching together for ways to meet not only their academic needs but also their physical, social, and emotional needs can be a challenge—but so very rewarding.

After 20 years of teaching, Judy has never felt better. She takes advantage of every possible opportunity to network and attend workshops. Sadly, her neighbor and fellow 20-year veteran, Theresa, is counting the years until retirement. Both teachers began their careers with such a zest for teaching and learning. Now one only "teaches," whereas the other continues to learn along the way as well.

Judy made some final comments and presented each guest with a final packet of materials. Handshakes and promises to keep in touch are exchanged. Dewey and Pine Lake have begun their partnership.

Questions for Discussion and Activities

1. What do you feel the next step should be for the Pine Lake faculty?
2. During the summary discussion, would it be appropriate for Judy McKay or other Dewey staff to mention any of their school's current shortcomings? Why or why not?

3. What are the advantages and disadvantages of teachers participating in released-time activities such as visitations?
4. What are other resources that a school contemplating the middle school concept could tap?
5. Research the role of the Internet as a possible resource tool.
6. Conduct an interview with the executive director or president of your state professional association for middle grade schools. What are the benefits of membership in such an organization?
7. Write to the National Middle School Association for information. What are the benefits of membership in a national association for middle grade schools?

Relationship to Turning Points Recommendations

- Empower teachers and administrators
- Prepare teachers for the middle grades

Recommended Reading

Slater, J. K. (1990). *Middle grades reform in California: Current and expected attainment of recommendation in "Caught in the middle." Interim evaluation* (Technical report). Sacramento: California Department of Education.

Slater, J. K. (1993). Using regional school networks to orchestrate reform in California middle school grades. *Elementary School Journal, 93*(5), 481-493.

Story 24:

Patty's Problem

"Wow, that was such a great party Friday night. I think it was the best one we've had all year. Patty sure was drunk. That was probably the drunkest I have ever seen her!" Mary exclaimed to her group of eighth-grade friends gathered in front of her locker on Monday morning.

"Yeah, Patty was pretty gone. She was sick the entire night after the party and when I left her house on Saturday morning, she was still getting sick," Jill replied. "Her mom was really worried because she couldn't understand why Patty was sick. Her mom has no idea her daughter is probably the biggest partyer in the eighth grade."

As Jill spoke, Patty came trudging down the hall toward her locker. She looked terrible. Her eyes had dark circles under them as if she had not slept in days. As she approached the group, Mark shouted, "How was the doctor? Was your mommy worried about you? You should have just told her that you were fine, just a bit hungover." As Mark finished his comments, Patty started to weep. No one knew what to say, until finally Jill asked her what was wrong.

Through her tears, Patty started to explain the rest of her horrible weekend to the group. "My mom was so worried about me Saturday morning that she took me to the doctor. I tried to explain to her that I was fine, that I just had a touch of the flu, but she wouldn't buy it, and she made me go. I knew exactly what was wrong with me, but I couldn't tell Mom that I was hungover because she would kill me. After the doctor ran a few tests, he came back in and brought my mom with him. He sat both of us down and told us the news. He stated that the reason I was so sick, on top of being drunk, was that I'm pregnant! I instantly began to cry and my mom's mouth dropped open. Neither one of us knew what to say. She took me home and we didn't say a single word to each other."

As Patty finished her story, the entire group was in shock, especially Jim, who everyone knew must be the father. No one said a word until Mark spoke up and said, "Oh, no, look at the time, it is almost eight. We had better get to class so we don't get sent to the office for another tardy." Jill and Molly both quickly agreed. Thinking they were now alone, Patty and Jim knew they had things to discuss.

Dumbfounded, Jim asked, "Are you sure you're pregnant?" Patty just nodded yes.

"Well, am I the father?" Patty couldn't answer, but once again nodded yes. As the 8 o'clock bell rang, they quietly walked off to their separate classes.

Though Patty and Jim were unaware of his presence, the counselor Ted Barrett had overheard their conversation, and as they turned to go to class, he hurried back to his office to regain his composure and to figure out what to do next.

Patty sat through Advisory with tears in her eyes and a blank stare on her face. Ever since she found out she was pregnant, she had been numb. Sunday, after her mom got over the shock, they sat down and tried to talk about the problem. That just made matters worse. All her mom wanted to know was how Patty could have been so dumb to have ever let something like that happen. She had grilled Patty to find out who the father was and how long she had been having sex. She never once tried to comfort her or offer advice.

Patty never thought that this could happen to her. She and Jim always used protection, well, except for that one time after Mark's party. They had both been pretty drunk, one thing led to another, and eventually they had, she recalled, laughed when they realized that neither of them had a condom. But never did they think that one time would matter. Numb, Patty just sat, letting class continue around her as if the others were all in another world.

Across the hall, Jim was also in a state of shock. He had just learned that he was going to be a father. "I'm too young to be a father," he kept saying to himself. "I never meant for this to happen. We were just having fun. I am going to get killed when I tell my parents what I have gotten myself into this time. This is the worst day of my life."

Meanwhile, back in his office, Ted Barrett contemplated his plan of action. He knew that Patty was mixed up with the wrong crowd, but he never expected it would result in a pregnancy. He knew he needed to call Patty in and try to talk to her before contacting her mother and trying to link the family to available services in the community.

When Patty entered the counselor's office, she was still weeping and looked like a lost, scared child rather than the adult she'd tried to be just yesterday. Ted Barrett and Patty did not know each other well, but Patty had heard others talk about how cool he was, and she felt hopeful.

"Is there anything wrong or anything you would like to talk about, Patty?" Ted Barrett asked. Patty just sat back in her chair and shook her head no.

"Well, Patty, I think there is something wrong," Ted said. "I can tell that you have been weeping. I also overheard you and Jim talking this morning in the hallway. I don't want you to think that I am being nosy, but I am here to listen and to offer help if you need it."

Patty started to weep even harder. She really did want to talk about it with somebody, but whenever she tried to talk she just wept harder. Ted Barrett leaned over and held Patty's hand until the weeping eased up. This show of compassion moved Patty and she slowly started to tell the story of her horrible weekend all over again.

By the time she was finished, Patty had begun to feel a bit better. Unlike her mom, Ted Barrett just listened and did not criticize. "Have you thought about what you are going to do about the baby?" he asked. Patty just sat there with a blank stare on her face. This had been the same question Patty had asked herself all weekend. And she didn't have a clue what the answer should be.

Questions for Discussion and Activities

1. What are some possible actions that Ted Barrett might suggest to Patty?
2. What are the legal issues regarding the actions of counselors, teachers, and administrators in situations like this?
3. What are some of the characteristics of young adolescents brought out in this story?
4. What are some things that can be done in the school to educate students about safe sex and pregnancy? What groups might oppose such activities in the school? What is your opinion on this issue?
5. Make a list of some local agencies in the community that could be involved in teaching the students about safe sex. Contact these agencies and conduct interviews to determine what role, if any, they have in working with schools on related health issues.

Relationship to Turning Points Recommendations

- Improve academic performance through better health and fitness
- Engage families
- Connect schools with communities

Recommended Reading

Elkind, D. (1978). Understanding the young adolescent. *Adolescence, 13*(49), 1-7.

Hillman, S., Wood, P., Becker, M., & Altier, D. (1990). Young adolescent risk-taking behavior: Theory, research and implications for middle schools. In J. Irvin (Ed.), *Research in middle level education: Selected studies 1990* (pp. 39-50). Columbus, OH: National Middle School Association.

Newcomb, M., & Bentler, P. (1989). Substance use and abuse among children and teenagers. *American Psychologist, 44,* 242-248.

Looking Forward 6

Story 25:

Summer, Here We Come

Jane Byers couldn't believe the end of the year had arrived. "It seems like just yesterday that the new school year began and all of our new students and teachers were making their way around Dewey. So many things have happened here this year, some bad, but mostly good. I still keep thinking about how wonderfully the Christmas service project went at Oakdale Manor. That was probably the best project ever. The kids were great and all of the teachers worked together to get it done. I wish everything would go that smoothly, but we are not that fortunate." Jane continued her mental review of the year's successes and failures as she waited for the final bell of the year to toll.

When the bell went off, the school seemed to erupt with the excitement that summer vacation brings each year. The hallway quickly filled with students rushing to their lockers for one last time.

"All right, summer, here we come! This summer is going to be great! Lots of time to party," Mark exclaimed to Jill, Molly, and Jim.

"Speak for yourself!" Jim replied, "I don't plan on doing much partying. My summer will be spent grounded in my house. Since my parents found out about Patty, I haven't been allowed to leave the house."

"Hey, man, I am sorry that the folks are treating you bad, but I guess you can't blame them. You did get Patty pregnant. At least you are better off than Patty. She has not had a moment of peace since her mom found out," Jill commented.

"Yeah, I guess you're right, things could be worse," Jim said. "I feel really bad for Patty. I wish there was something I could do to help. Her mom won't even let me talk to her."

"Well, hopefully, we have all learned from what happened to Patty. I know that I am more careful now," Molly commented as Ted Barrett walked by.

Down the hall, Lisa and Kathy were talking to Ken Wilson about another matter entirely. "But, Mr. Wilson, there is no way that I deserved a B in science. I have made straight As all my life. How can you do this to me? Do you realize that you have ruined my summer? All I can think about is how I got a B. Can't you change it, even to an A−?" Lisa pleaded.

"No, Lisa, I gave you a B because you earned a B. It would not be fair to you or any of the other students if I raised your grade to an A. There is still nothing wrong with a B," Ken Wilson replied.

"Speak for yourself!" Lisa exclaimed. "A B is horrible. I might as well get an F. They are the same in my book." It would be a while before summer fun really started for Lisa. But across the hall, the fun had already begun.

"Are you about ready to get going?" Matt asked. "By the time we get to the park all of the courts will be taken." "I'll be done in a minute, but I told Sarah that I would wait for her by my locker and she could come with us, so hold on just a second. There will still be a court available when we get there," Steve replied.

Just then, Sarah and Christy walked up. "All right, let's get out of here. I am ready for summer," Sarah exclaimed.

"I am with you on that one," Christy said. "Summer could not have come any sooner. I am so glad that next year we will not be the youngest ones in the school. It got really old being the youngest ones in school.

Seventh grade has to be better than sixth because if it isn't, then next year is going to be very bad."

"Aw, Christy, this year was not that bad," Sarah commented.

"Speak for yourself," retorted Christy, still hoping that next year would be better.

"Are we just going to stand here and complain, or are we going to go enjoy the summer?" Matt asked. "Let's get out of this place!"

The hallways quickly emptied and the Dewey teachers, who had been out saying good-bye to their charges, broke into wide smiles as they realized that they too were ready for summer to begin.

Next year would be different at Dewey Middle School. Some of the staff would be on different teams and some would not return at all. There would be new plans, new projects, and new students.

Some of the teachers worried about losing Jane Byers when they learned that the principalship at the new elementary school in the district had been posted; others, including Richard Hoff, hoped she'd bid out.

One thing was for sure. This summer would go quickly, as summers do. So all of the Dewey staff proceeded to their classrooms to finish closing out so they would be on time for the official summer kickoff party to be held at Ed Matzler's house later that afternoon. There was a lot to celebrate about the past year and they were anxious to get started.

Questions for Discussion and Activities

1. What characteristics of young adolescents were brought out in this story?
2. What stereotypes of young adolescents did you identify in the story?
3. Review the literature on year-round schools. In light of your knowledge of the characteristics of young adolescents, develop a position statement about the need for year-round schooling with appropriate support from the literature.
4. How can communities support young adolescents during off-school hours, both during the school year and during vacation periods?
   a. What are healthy alternatives for off-school activities?
   b. What responsibility do the school and community have to provide students with options for recreation and leisure activities during off-school hours?
   c. Design a program to meet young adolescents' needs for recreation, fitness, and socialization.

5. Interview several teachers to find out how they typically spend summer vacation.

Relationship to Turning Points *Recommendations*

- Prepare teachers for the middle level
- Improve academic performance through better health and fitness
- Connect schools with communities

Recommended Reading

George, P., & Alexander, W. (1993). *The exemplary middle school.* New York: Harcourt Brace Jovanovich.

George, P., Stevenson, C., Thomason, J., & Beane, J. (1992). *The middle school and beyond.* Alexandria, VA: Association for Supervision and Curriculum Development.

Raebeck, B. (1992). *Transforming middle schools: A guide to whole-school change.* Lancaster, PA: Technomic.

Epilogue

You have finished your journey with us at Dewey Middle School. We have tried to give you a sampling of issues that can emerge as middle schools evolve—issues related to teaming, flexible scheduling, advisory groups, inclusion, the role of nonacademic subjects, cultural diversity, parent involvement, evaluation, the role of the community, and the ever-challenging behavior of the young adolescent.

If we look into the future at Dewey, we may see the following scenarios for Dewey and those who made up the Dewey culture. And although whimsical, all things, after all, are possible.

- Dewey became a nationally recognized middle school. Visitors from all over the world came on a daily basis. A new position had to be created to handle public relations.
- Principal Jane Byers stayed at Dewey 4 more years and then moved out of state to become the administrator for a Horace Mann School of the Future.
- Assistant Principal Richard Hoff retired on schedule, after becoming a strong advocate for middle school philosophy. Two years before he retired, he was president of the state middle school

association. He was asked to be the principal at Dewey, but he decided he would rather retire and fish in the Caribbean.

- Counselor Ted Barrett left teaching and became a stockbroker. The nickname, "Spot" was pinned on him because of his acumen at spotting good deals for his clients.
- Priscilla Mac remained a special education resource teacher at Dewey for 25 years.
- Bill Morris, basketball coach, took a leave of absence during that awful year when the basketball players went on strike. He was chosen as a replacement for the Dallas Mavericks, but he only played in three games before the strike was over and the replacements were politely asked to hang up their jerseys. Bill, however, didn't want to leave the great state of Texas, so he opened a sports bar in Hickory Creek.
- Emily Pritchart, language arts teacher, remained an enthusiastic teacher and a loyal supporter of Dewey until she retired.
- Sharon Becker, the best teacher at Dewey, wrote a book on teaching and became a nationally renowned speaker and advocate for teachers.
- Martha Docweiler went to Greece one summer and never returned.

As for the Dewey students—

- Patty kept her baby, later received her GED, went to college, got her Ph.D., and is teaching psychology at a southern Illinois university.
- Sonia finished high school, married, had two children, and teaches Sunday school.
- Jill is in the entertainment business. She is a frequent guest on a variety of daytime talk shows.
- Jim became a car salesman.
- Johnny never did make it to the Olympics, but went on to become a golf pro at the local country club.
- Claire never finished high school and is raising five children while her husband tries not to get fired by his most recent employer for drinking on the job. She sees Lisa, who is a family systems counselor in Oakdale, on a regular basis.

Teachers, administrators, and students are always changing, and as they change, their stories change. Becoming a middle school is, after all, a never-ending process. It is a journey with no final destination, a beginning with no end. Strategic transitions will continually be needed in schools so they can respond to the ever-changing needs of young adolescents. Decisions will need to be made at critical turning points in a school's development, which like ours, is a journey that never really ends.

CORWIN
PRESS

The Corwin Press logo—a raven striding across an open book—represents the happy union of courage and learning. We are a professional-level publisher of books and journals for K-12 educators, and we are committed to creating and providing resources that embody these qualities. Corwin's motto is "Success for All Learners."